Maya Lin, Public Art, and the Confluence Project

I0473500

The first scholarly monograph devoted exclusively to this vital work of contemporary public art, this book examines Maya Lin's Confluence Project through the lens of environmental humanities and Indigenous studies.

Matthew Reynolds provides a detailed analysis of each earthwork, along with a discussion of the proposed final project at Celilo Falls near The Dalles, Oregon. The book assesses the artist's longtime engagement with the region of the Pacific Northwest and explores the Confluence Project within Lin's larger oeuvre. Several consistent themes and experiences are common among all the sites. These include an emphasis on individual, multisensory encounters with the earthworks and their surrounding contexts; sound as an experiential dimension of landscape; indexical accounts of the multicultural, multispecies histories of each place; and an evocation of loss.

The book will be of interest to scholars working in art history, contemporary art, environmental studies, environmental humanities, and Native American studies.

Matthew Reynolds is Associate Professor in the Department of Art History and Visual Culture Studies at Whitman College, Walla Walla, Washington.

Routledge Focus on Art History and Visual Studies

Routledge Focus on Art History and Visual Studies presents short-form books on varied topics within the fields of art history and visual studies.

Post-Digital Letterpress Printing
Research, Education and Practice
Edited by Pedro Manuel Reis Amado, Ana Catarina Silva and Vítor Quelhas

Bodily Engagements with Film, Images, and Technology
Somavision
Max Ryynänen

Performance, Art and Politics in the African Diaspora
Necropolitics and the Black Body
Myron M. Beasley

Contemporary Art, Systems, and the Aesthetics of Dispersion
Francis Halsall

A Philosophy of Cultural Scenes in Art and Popular Culture
Max Ryynänen and Jozef Kovalčik

Translation and Transgression in the Art of Shirin Neshat
Erin C. Devine

Maya Lin, Public Art, and the Confluence Project
Matthew Reynolds

For more information about this series, please visit: https://www.routledge.com/ Routledge-Focus-on-Art-History-and-Visual-Studies/book-series/FOCUSAH

Maya Lin, Public Art, and the Confluence Project

Matthew Reynolds

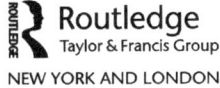

Routledge
Taylor & Francis Group
NEW YORK AND LONDON

First published 2024
by Routledge
605 Third Avenue, New York, NY 10158

and by Routledge
4 Park Square, Milton Park, Abingdon, Oxon, OX14 4RN

Routledge is an imprint of the Taylor & Francis Group, an informa business

Library of Congress Cataloging-in-Publication Data
Title: Maya Lin, public art, and the Confluence Project / Matthew Reynolds.
Description: New York, NY : Routledge, 2024. | Includes bibliographical references and index.
Identifiers: LCCN 2023055895 (print) | LCCN 2023055896 (ebook) |
ISBN 9781032288123 (hardback) | ISBN 9781032312927 (paperback) |
ISBN 9781003309024 (ebook)
Subjects: LCSH: Lin, Maya, 1959- Confluence. | Lin, Maya, 1959---Criticism and interpretation. | Public art--Columbia River Valley. | Site-specific art--Columbia River Valley. | Art and society--Columbia River Valley.
Classification: LCC N6537.L54 A63 2024 (print) |
LCC N6537.L54 (ebook) | DDC 700.9797--dc23/eng/20231215
LC record available at https://lccn.loc.gov/2023055895
LC ebook record available at https://lccn.loc.gov/2023055896

ISBN: 978-1-032-28812-3 (hbk)
ISBN: 978-1-032-31292-7 (pbk)
ISBN: 978-1-003-30902-4 (ebk)

DOI: 10.4324/9781003309024

Typeset in Times New Roman
by KnowledgeWorks Global Ltd.

For Mom, Marilyn, reader, writer, teacher.

For Mika, for a more sustainable future.

Contents

Figures

Acknowledgments

First and foremost, I wish to thank the Confluence Project directors and staff, past and present, for their continued efforts to promote this endlessly fascinating public art project. It is a foundation upon which to build a more just, equitable, and sustainable world. Somehow, the language of "justice and equitability" has become controversial at this current historical moment. This book attempts to answer in its own way the reasons behind that "somehow." That our seemingly intractable national divisions are aligned with the current climate crisis and are deeply interconnected.

I am grateful to Confluence Executive Director Colin Fogarty for his support throughout this research project. A seemingly casual conversation about what the organization might do with its administrative records led to Confluence's remarkable donation of this material to Whitman College and Northwest Archives. In addition to administrative files, the gift includes blueprints and design proposals, education files, press clippings, audiovisual materials, and maquettes. My thanks to the many other Confluence staff members, especially Program Manager Courtney Yilk and Editorial and Content Manager Lily Hart, who have given generously of their time and extensive knowledge as I've undertaken additional research for this book. The Confluence Project website was a rich resource. I urge those interested in Lin's work and the history of the region's first inhabitants to utilize the wealth of material available there.

Maya Lin's involvement is due primarily to the influence of Antone Minthorn, former Chairman of the Confederated Tribes of the Umatilla Indian Reservation (CTUIR) and current Board Chair of Confluence Project. A Vietnam veteran, he was moved by the Lin-designed memorial in Washington, DC. The vision for Confluence that unfolded would commemorate Lewis and Clark's cross-continent journey without monumentalizing the figures. Working collaboratively with former Confluence Executive Director Jane Jacobsen, former director of the Washington State Historical Society David Nicandri, and many others, the intention was to demythologize the Corps of Discovery's expedition. It was in many ways a heroic journey, but the role of Native American Indigenous peoples is all-too-frequently overlooked or forgotten—still to this day. Indians helped feed the crew, shared their geographical knowledge, at times provided shelter and protection, and were partners in trade, sometimes adversaries but always ever-present in their own homelands. Confluence attempts to rectify this historic oversight through a design program that calls attention to the histories, rituals, and lifeways that have been lost or suppressed by settler colonialism but were never lost to Native Americans themselves. I wish also to acknowledge the vital role of Roberta "Bobbie" Conner, Executive Director of the Tamástlikt Cultural Institute in Pendleton, Oregon. She, too, was a guiding presence for Confluence, and I have learned greatly from my interactions with her over the years.

Whitman College has supported this project through multiple stages. A year-long sabbatical in 2022–2023 provided the space and breathing room for more focused research and writing time. I am grateful to the many students who contributed to this research in my classes, including Art Since 1945 and Art/Environment. Over two iterations of the latter class, students used archival records to plan and prepare for an exhibition held at Whitman's Maxey Museum in 2021. Maxey Museum Director Libby Miller and Sheehan Gallery Director and Collections Manager Kynde Kiefel brought expertise and professionalism of a kind that would benefit any museum anywhere, much less a rural, small, private liberal arts college. Audrey Mace, Camille Marshall, and Melina Waldman were instrumental in the show's realization. The resulting exhibition was profiled in the *New York Times* in a special section devoted to art in a post-pandemic world—a thrill for everyone involved.

Whitman Archives staff, past and present, have been amazing collaborators over the past seven years. When the opportunity to house Confluence materials was brought to then-director Melissa Salrin, there was no hesitation on her part, only excitement and encouragement. Ben Murphy stepped into the role of director and guided the collection to its new home with the help of Amy Blau, Scholarly Communication Librarian and U-Haul driver extraordinaire. Once on campus, Dana Bronson made sure the material was processed and cataloged in a timely manner. Joel Gaytan and West Bales fulfilled endless requests for pulling boxes and scanning documents and design plans. Whitman College supported a series of student assistants to facilitate this work and research at every stage. I'm forever grateful to Emma Phillips, Laura Rivale, Audrey Mace (again), Rachel Glaser, and Anna Stone for helping me dig through boxes, pore over records, watch video, and examine and interpret images. Their efforts were instrumental in the realization of this project. I wish also to give credit and praise to Kelsey Martin, Community Learning Specialist, my co-chair of the Community Engaged Learning and Research Initiative during a global pandemic and austerity cuts at Whitman College. Kelsey helped me see the broader connections between my research and the surrounding communities with whom it is concerned.

Finally, I wish to thank my friends, colleagues, and family who provided encouragement, intellectual engagement, laughter, and solace during the long gestation of this book. My departmental colleagues, Krista Gulbransen and Lisa Uddin, read chapter drafts and offered invaluable feedback. Tim Parker provided insight about birds, biology, and geology—terrain with which I was much less familiar. Katherine Barber generously spoke with students about the agonies and indomitability of the lives of the people of the Columbia River Plateau and beyond and how they were forever changed by the disappearance of Celilo Falls. Ken Allan invited me to speak about this work on several different occasions, helping to legitimize the project in my own mind. Regular meetings with Emily Washines (about a related project yet to come to fruition) provided greater context and insight into Native experiences in the region. Dennis Crockett and Susan Babilon hosted me for an informal writer's retreat at their house in Waldport, Oregon, overlooking Wakanda Beach. Thank you for gin and tonics on the deck, board games at the dinner table, a comfy room, laughter, insight, wisdom, and friendship. When lockdown began, Dave McCoy and Mark Bowen reached out through an ever-evolving text thread that may ultimately achieve literary merit equal to anything I have written here. Thanks especially to Leesa and Mika, my partner and daughter, my life. You are both in this book in more ways than I think you can know. Sorry. And you're welcome.

This book is about a series of public artworks, a topic with which I am very familiar. But it is also about Lewis and Clark, Indigenous cultures, climate change, and the Columbia River Plateau—topics about which I knew little before I arrived in Walla Walla in 2008. I've followed the lead of the Confluence Project in the use of terminology associated with Native American, Indian, and Indigenous places and people for consistency's sake. As a straight White male scholar, this book may (ironically) seem like an incursion into territories in which I am unwelcome. Despite my best efforts, I'm fairly confident I will have gotten a few things wrong, misrepresented views, and/or misidentified people or communities for whom history is alive in their daily struggles for recognition and acceptance. For that, I offer my apologies, welcome corrections, and humbly ask for forgiveness. There are over two centuries of atonement required by the likes of me. I hope this book can mark a small step in the right direction.

Introduction

In 1999, Maya Lin was invited by a group of arts patrons working in collaboration with Indigenous tribes of the Columbia River Plateau and Pacific Northwest to commemorate the then-forthcoming bicentennial of the Lewis and Clark expedition. The concept that developed was a series of seven earthworks to be built along the Columbia and Snake Rivers. It would be called the Confluence Project. Each location was determined by its historical relevance to the 1804–1806 Corps of Discovery's journey and its significance to the Native American tribes of the Plateau region.

Lin's lifelong interest in the environment also meant that sites were chosen for their ecological value. For example, Cape Disappointment is not only the endpoint of the Corps of the Discovery's westward expedition, it is the place where the Columbia meets the Pacific Ocean. This vital estuary is home to coastal tribes and a transit point for salmon—a unique habitat for this anadromous species, one of the few that can exist in both salt and freshwater. Salmon are both a fundamental food source for all tribal communities of the Pacific Northwest and inland Plateau and a foundational cultural touchstone. Life revolves around and with this once-abundant species. Similarly, the confluence of the Snake and Columbia Rivers outside of Pasco, Washington, was a crucial point of contact for Plateau peoples, a meeting place, a place for trade and communication, games and negotiations, and the sharing of stories, rituals, and traditions for over 10,000 years. It was also a place where Lewis and Clark were warmly welcomed by the Nez Perce and other tribes, and given food, shelter, and safety to recover after a grueling phase of their journey.

Maya Lin's involvement was the inspiration of many people, but it was Antone Minthorn, then-Chairman of the Confederated Tribes of the Umatilla Indian Reservation (CTUIR), who was key to her participation. Minthorn is a veteran of the Vietnam War and was deeply moved by Lin's memorial, built on the Mall in Washington, DC, and dedicated in 1981. The members of the bicentennial planning committee were unanimously opposed to a monument to Lewis and Clark or anything that had even a faint scent of celebrating Manifest

DOI: 10.4324/9781003309024-1

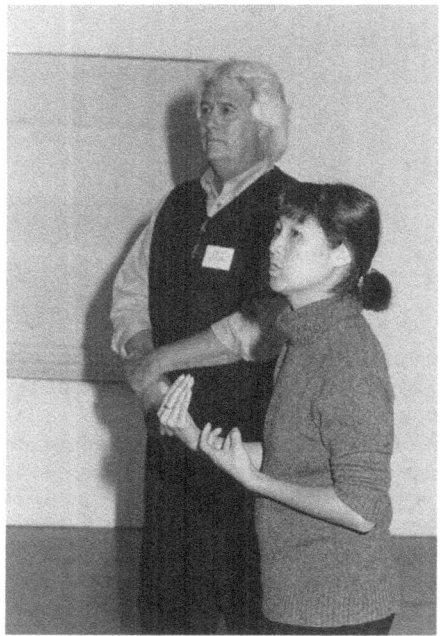

Figure 0.1 Johnpaul Jones (left) and Maya Lin (right) discussing Confluence Project at the Portland Art Museum, April 16, 2002.

Sources: Photo by Lynette Johnson. Box 3, Folder 40. WCMss444. Confluence Project Records. Whitman College and Northwest Archives.

Destiny. Minthorn, Washington State Historical Society director David Nicandri, and Jane Jacobsen from the Vancouver National Historic Reserve Trust agreed that Lin would be an ideal choice to produce a series of artworks along the Columbia River. But Lin was hesitant, wary of making something that might be interpreted as another memorial or that further entrenched the damaging stereotype of Native Americans as relics of the past. After more than a year of negotiation and follow-up requests, Lin agreed to take on the project in 2002. Their shared vision originally called for seven public art installations at state parks along the Columbia and Snake Rivers. To date, five earthworks have been built at Cape Disappointment State Park at the mouth of the Columbia near Astoria, Oregon; Fort Vancouver, Washington; Sandy River Delta, near the Columbia River Gorge outside of Portland, Oregon; Sacajawea State Park, at the convergence of the Snake and Columbia and just south of Pasco, Washington; and Chief Timothy Park, on the Snake River near the border of Idaho and Washington (Figure 0.1). Designs for a sixth site at Celilo Park, near

The Dalles, Oregon, have been completed, but at the time of this writing, the project has been indefinitely suspended. (Banse 2019) Plans for a seventh site had to be abandoned after the financial crisis of 2008.

Each location foregrounds the histories and cultures of Native Americans. Lewis and Clark's journal entries written at or near the Confluence sites are a strong reminder that the land they set out to "discover" was already occupied by scores of Indigenous communities. For over a month, journal entries between October and November of 1805 describe daily encounters with small groups of Indians, descriptions of "houses" and small villages, larger encampments, and even what might today be called marinas filled with canoes floating near shore. "This is the first night which we have been entirely clear of Indians since our arrival on the waters of the Columbia River," Clark wrote on November 4th. (Meriwether Lewis, William Clark, et al., November 4, 1805 entry in The Journals of the Lewis and Clark Expedition, ed. Gary Moulton 2005.) The earthworks and installations present the more complex stories of the daily lives and rituals of the region's diverse inhabitants by creating spaces that reanimate those same stories through text, pictographs, references to species and topography, and Indigenous myths.

Prior to settler contact, each site represented a vastly important symbolic and social space for the continent's first inhabitants. The exact location of many of those places now lies underwater, inundated by the 41 dams of the Columbia and Snake Rivers. Perhaps most valuable of all, the Confluence Project works to burst the stubborn myth of *Indians as history*, the vanishing race depicted in the photographs of Edward Curtis or the nostalgic artwork of Frederic Remington. An often-neglected aspect of Confluence is its educational outreach programs and its ongoing mission of "connecting people to the history, living cultures, and ecology" of the Columbia and Snake River systems. The Confluence earthworks are more than passive viewing experiences; they are active pedagogical spaces, asking viewers to see, hear, smell, and fathom the vast changes of two centuries of industrial development. For Confluence is also about the dispossession of lands and eradication of lifeways that enabled the current ecological crisis and species extinctions we are living through in the present moment.

For more than three decades, Maya Lin's body of work has emphasized issues of sustainability and an engagement with environmental conservation. She states that her sculptures, installations, earthworks, and architecture are "inspired by landscape, topography, and natural phenomena but it's a landscape from a twenty-first-century perspective, a landscape through the lens of technology." (Lin 2000, 12:06-12:07) Scholarly analyses similarly focus on the interconnectedness between Lin's sculptures, installations, and ecological concerns. William Fox, Director of the Center for Art + Environment at the Nevada Museum of Art, states that her work demonstrates "how her relationships to natural and built environments are interwoven in a long-standing research-based practice…She demands, without ever uttering a polemic, that we pay attention and fix stuff." (Fox 2015, 355) Critic Susette Min adds that "A major portion of Lin's recent work…centers on the environmental impact of global warming on the earth." (Min 2009) Lin's work asks viewers to be aware of a broader ecological framework, one that enfolds her built projects. To better understand the Confluence Project requires careful attention to the works themselves, as well as the architectural, infrastructural, and human-made surroundings at each location.

All of these sites occupy or evoke the rural landscapes of the Pacific Northwest.[1] But these are not the pastoral idylls so commonly associated with the countryside. Instead, contemporary rural spaces are carefully planned and managed by a host of industries: agriculture, energy, livestock, manufacturing, trade, and tourism. Art critic Lucy Lippard writes: "Out on the margins, where local scars cover for global perpetrators, we live in a distorted mirror image of the center, which perceives our 'nature' as primarily resource. Here negative space can be more important than what's constructed from its deported materials elsewhere." (Lippard 2014, 10) Negative space is a term borrowed from sculpture and implies spatial emptiness but is, in fact, highly developed. Negative space coexists with its positive counterpart—the one entirely dependent on and imbricated within the other.

This book will provide an overview of the five extant sites of Maya Lin's Confluence Project, along with a discussion of the plans for the sixth installation at Celilo Falls National Park. In so doing, it will situate these within a longer timeframe of Indigenous habitation. Lewis and Clark were among the first wave of settler colonists foretold by Indian prophecies. This book will examine those initial encounters, as well as the long history of violence and genocide that followed in their wake. It will illustrate how the earthworks of the Confluence Project address the transformation of the natural environment over the last two centuries and call attention to the urgency of our current ecological crisis. It will situate Lin's body of work within a longer genealogy of public art, rooted in Minimalism and Conceptualism's emphasis on artistic engagement with its unique location: its site-specificity, its use of language as both representational device and its capacity for place-making, and Confluence's unique dialogic dimensions that emphasize the Project's educational and community outreach initiatives. Throughout, the book will examine how the Confluence Project deliberately engages and incorporates its surrounding environments. It will demonstrate how the art is entangled with the industrialized geographies it occupies, calling attention to a broader ecological framework. Ultimately, it will argue that the Confluence Project offers a poignant recognition of the interconnectedness of "negative" and "positive," urban and rural, humanity and environment, past and present. It has much to tell us at this historical moment—a moment in which large-scale ecological disaster can no longer be denied, but also a moment in which we cannot collectively seem to find the will or the way to address it.

Finally, I wish to highlight the unique archival foundation of this book. In 2018, Whitman College acquired Confluence Project archival materials, including maquettes, site surveys and records, blueprints and other architectural plans, documents related to educational outreach and programming, interviews with tribal members of the region, photos, newsletters, and much more. (WCMss444, "Confluence Project records", Whitman College and Northwest Archives) These records were initially planned to be housed at the Columbia River Center, a multipurpose exhibition and study center that was to serve as the seventh, and final, Confluence site. The building was to be constructed near the city of Vancouver, Washington, and its mission would be devoted to the health of the Columbia River. But, like so many great ideas, it was ultimately sacrificed to the fickle gods of finance capital during the Great Recession of 2008.

This remarkable collection of records has provided enormous insight into what I believe is one of the most complex and ambitious public art projects ever. To put this in perspective, Confluence could be characterized as one of the largest artworks in history if measured in the 438-mile distance between Chief Timothy Park and Cape Disappointment, rather than the individual footprints of each site. A process that began over two decades ago may be complete. Or it may still have one more site to build. Either way, the educational work in schools and communities is ongoing, complicating a date of completion and extending the work's lifespan indefinitely. It was also extremely expensive. Final budget estimates place the cost at around $35 million. Lin accepted reduced fees for her participation, and the project's high price should also account for the major infrastructural improvements that happened alongside the art's installation. That Confluence did not always succeed in its initial goals, or that plans had to adjust to the realities of working with state and federal agencies, tribal nations and councils, city governments, nonprofits, private patrons, contractors, landscape designers, and the myriad other entities who contributed should not be viewed as a sign of failure. These records instead document a remarkable series of achievements and provide the source for what I hope will bring new insights into the work of Maya Lin, public art, and the Confluence Project.

Note

1 The term landscape has a very rich body of literature associated with it. The word's origins are explicitly art historical. It was coined specifically to describe depictions of oil paintings of Dutch countryside popular in the 1500s. While this history is vital to understanding the deployment of "landscape" and its affiliation as a descriptor for rural spaces, the broader debates around its usage are outside the scope of this project. For further reading on the topic, please see W.J.T. Mitchell, *Landscape and Power* (Chicago, IL: University of Chicago Press, 2002), John Berger and Tom Overton, ed., *Landscape and Art* (New York, NY: Verso, 2016), and Deborah Bright, "Of Mother Nature and Marlboro Men: An Inquiry Into the Cultural Meanings of Landscape Photography," in Richard Bolton, ed., *The Contest of Meaning: Critical Histories of Photography* (Cambridge, MA: MIT Press, 1989).

References

Banse, Tom. 2019. "Columbia River Art Installation at The Dalles Put on Hold by Yakama Nation Opposition." Northwest Public Broadcasting. Accessed February 10, 2019. https://www.nwpb.org/2019/02/09/columbia-river-art-installation-at-the-dalles-put-on-hold-by-yakama-nation-opposition/

"Confluence Project Records", WCMss444, Whitman College and Northwest Archives. https://archiveswest.orbiscascade.org/ark:/80444/xv285430

Fox, William. 2015. *Maya Lin: Topologies*. New York, NY: Rizzoli.

Lewis, Meriwether, Clark, William, et al. September 4, 1806 entry in The Journals of the Lewis and Clark Expedition, ed. Gary Moulton. Lincoln, NE: University of Nebraska Press / University of Nebraska-Lincoln Libraries-Electronic Text Center, 2005. http://lewisandclarkjournals.unl.edu/journals.php?id=1806-09-04.

Lin, Maya. 2000. *Boundaries*. New York, NY: Simon & Schuster.

Lippard, Lucy R. 2014. *Undermining: A Wild Ride through Land Use, Politics, and Art in the Changing West*. New York, NY: The New Press.

Min, Susette. 2009. "Entropic Designs: A Review of Maya Lin: Systematic Landscapes and Asian/American/Modern Art: Shifting Currents, 1900–1970 at the de Young Museum." *American Quarterly* 61 (1): 193–215. https://doi.org/10.1353/aq.0.0056

1 Cape Disappointment State Park

"We start where Lewis and Clark's journey ended at the mouth of the Columbia, where the river meets the sea, holding up a mirror to reflect back upon
Lewis and Clark's journey." This quote from Maya Lin can be found on the
Confluence Project's webpage for the Cape Disappointment site. It was used
in much of the promotional literature shared with potential donors, educators,
and the public. Lin herself uttered the passage during the site's dedication
ceremony and in numerous public talks during the first few years following
its completion. This brief historiographical sketch is not meant as an indict-
ment of the quote's overuse. Instead, I want to acknowledge its metaphorical
potency. If the art installations at Cape Disappointment specifically, and the
Confluence Project more broadly, hold a mirror up to Lewis and Clark's journey, what might we see in its reflection? The Corps of Discovery's goal was
to reach the Pacific Ocean, and in that way, it is correct to say that the journey
"ended." But after a harsh winter that saw the crew build a small fortification
near a southern tributary of the Columbia—Fort Clatsop—they awaited the
coming of spring for the return trip back to St. Louis, at the time, the West-
ernmost edge of the United States and only recently acquired through the
Louisiana Purchase. It could only be the expedition's completion that would
allow the dissemination of the scientific, geographic, and cultural knowledge
accumulated along the way, information about Indian nations and their potential for commercial trade partnerships, and the mapping of the "most direct
& practicable water communication across this continent," in the words of
Thomas Jefferson. (DeVoto 1953, 482)

Lin's quote implies much more about the importance of the place of the
Columbia River estuary and what has happened since Lewis and Clark, however. The "we" who look into the mirror are contemporary viewers who see
not only a historic journey from two centuries ago but also the expansion of a
nation, the violent displacement and genocidal atrocities committed against the
land's first inhabitants, and the progress and growth of industrial technologies
that ushered in incredible advancements in energy, agriculture, commerce, and
trade. What do "we" see in this mirror reflection? Is it an image of a nation made
whole by Manifest Destiny, a country that has reached its inevitable potential?

DOI: 10.4324/9781003309024-2

Or is the mirror image reversed—a backward world in which progress and potential have brought us perilously close to environmental collapse. Hidden in Lin's exhortation is not just a request to think about the Corps of the Discovery. She is also asking us to consider the consequences of that quest and what has occurred in the more than two centuries since it took place.

Like the Confluence Project itself, this book begins with Cape Disappointment. It will provide an overview of the installations at the mouth of the Columbia River. It will discuss the region's first peoples, who inhabited this place for thousands of years prior to Lewis and Clark and who helped the members of the Corps survive a brutal winter in unfamiliar terrain. While Euro-American exploration and contact between traders and Native Americans had occurred well before Lewis and Clark's arrival, it can also be said that their voyage signaled a new phase in the ecological transformation of the region. As such, the chapter will also examine how the Confluence Project is an environmental work of art, and what it means to use that designation when discussing it. Despite Lin's lifelong dedication to ecological sustainability and the scenic setting of the five extant installations, visitors unfamiliar with the Confluence Project might be forgiven for failing to note an overt environmental focus. Nowhere do these works of art urge adoption of a vigorous conservation program, explain the science and damage of releasing carbon into the atmosphere, or provide facts about the catastrophic consequences to all life systems with a rise of more than 1.5 degrees C in global temperatures—a goal that the Intergovernmental Panel on Climate Change (IPCC) acknowledges is unattainable if carbon emissions continue at the current rate. ("AR6 Synthesis Report: Summary for Policymakers Headline Statements" 2023) You won't encounter any of the stereotypes about environmentalism that have so divided the nation over the past few decades: exhortations to recycle, abandon gas-guzzling vehicles, reduce waste or plastic consumption, and take up a plant-based diet. Only one artwork, the Bird Blind at Sandy River Delta, explicitly references species decline and extinction. This absence of didacticism is critical to understanding Confluence. To quote another phrase that has become axiomatic of Lin's work: "I create spaces to think, without trying to dictate what to think." (Box 3, Folder 55, "Confluence Project Records", WCMss444, Whitman College and Northwest Archives)

Chinook Encounters

Anthropologist Jon Daehnke describes the Lower Columbia as one of the most densely populated regions in Indigenous North America. "The Chinookan population…had a greater population density than nearly anywhere else in Indigenous North America north of Mexico." (Daehnke 2017, 36) The Chinookan village of Cathlapotle was the largest of a cluster of settlements located where the Lewis River, Gee Creek, and Lake River enter the Columbia near the present-day city of Ridgefield, Washington. ("Archaeology at Cathlapotle" 2016) Collaborative archeological excavations led by teams from the Chinook Nation and Portland State University in the 1990s found evidence of a continuously occupied cedar plank house dating back to 1400, but evidence of human presence in the Pacific Northwest extends back at least 12,000 years. (Box 3, Folder 55, Confluence Project Records, WCMss444, Whitman College and Northwest Archives)

Signs of contact between Chinook tribes and non-Natives date back to the seventeenth century. The Spanish had explored the coast as far north as Alaska prior to the British and French competition for furs that began more regular incursions into the region in the late eighteenth century. The Columbia River and Cape Disappointment took their Anglicized names from Capt. Robert Gray, who sailed his ship the *Columbia Rediva* into the mouth of the river in 1792 and was met by a large party of Chinook eager to expand their trade opportunities. (Daehnke, 2017, 40–41) A few years later, an expedition led by George Vancouver charted the Columbia as far inland as Portland. These early examples of contact between Native Americans and Europeans complicate the myth of Manifest Destiny. They are reminders that settler colonialism began on the coasts and moved inland well before larger groups of American migrants began to traverse the long and treacherous Oregon Trail.

The Columbia was the most important thoroughfare of the region both before and after settler contact. Evidence of this trade appears throughout Lewis and Clark's journals. Clark's entry for November 6, 1805, describes an encounter with an Indian who "Spoke a fiew words of English…" and told them of a "Mr. Haley" who carried forged iron objects in his canoe. (Lewis, et al., November 6, 1805 entry in The Journals of the Lewis and Clark Expedition 2005) Elsewhere they describe materials—blue and red colored beads and dyed fabrics, iron and metal tools and weapons—which had moved beyond novelty value and been fully integrated into Native cultures. Contact with explorers and settlers also brought with it devastating diseases, including smallpox, measles, influenza, malaria, and sexually transmitted diseases then unknown to Indians of the Pacific Northwest. Scholars note that deadly outbreaks affected most, if not all, of the Indigenous American populations, and that the Lower Columbia likely served as one of the primary disease vectors. Devastating smallpox outbreaks in 1792 and 1801 killed half of the Indigenous population of the Lower Columbia by the time of Lewis and Clark's arrival at Cape Disappointment. By the 1830s, it is estimated that as much as 90 percent of the Chinook and Cowlitz populations of the Willamette Valley had died from infection. (Hunn 1990, 27–32)

Disease and death continued to ravage Indian populations well into the nineteenth century. The losses faced by Chinookan tribes were compounded during the Treaty Era of the mid-nineteenth century. The federal government sought to relocate all Indians onto reservations east of the Cascades. During negotiations with Isaac Stevens, the appointed Governor of the Washington Territory and Superintendent of Indian Affairs, tribal delegates walked out when asked to abandon their ancestral homelands and relocate to different lands alongside numerous other regional bands, some of whom had been longtime adversaries. The loss of federal recognition was fought in the courts throughout the twentieth century and is still ongoing. During this period, the Chinook, like nearly all Native American tribes, were subject to systematic governmental policies that are best labeled a program of cultural genocide. Forced relocation, government-sanctioned theft of children to be indoctrinated into Western ways at abusive boarding schools, policies that forbade the speaking of Native languages or the practice of religion and high rates of addiction and suicide are all legacies of the shameful American colonial project. ("A Lower Columbia Chinook Historical Timeline" n.d.)

According to Daehnke, the Chinook Indian Nation "remain a close-knit and active community and are well known and respected by both the local non-Native community and Native tribes throughout the Pacific Northwest." (Daehnke, 2017, 60) In 2001, outgoing Assistant Secretary of Indian Affairs, Kevin Gover, granted federal recognition to the Chinook Indian Nation, an act that was almost immediately rescinded under the George W. Bush administration. Such recognition would restore treaty rights to fish and hunt, and make the tribe eligible for federal funds to address many of the problems listed above. If the Confluence Project's physical manifestation at Cape Disappointment is to be understood as a mirror reflecting not only Lewis and Clark's journey but the two centuries of development, much of which was predicated on the removal and eradication of Indian populations, this brief historical overview of the Lower Columbia's original inhabitants is a crucial first step in understanding Lin's artwork.

"Three Art Areas"

From the outset, Lin planned installations near Waikiki Beach facing the Pacific Ocean, and the east-looking interior inlet of Baker Bay. An early design plan produced by Maya Lin Studios in June 2004 lists "three art areas" to be built on opposite sides of the southward descending peninsula of Cape Disappointment State Park. "Artwork # 1" was described as a "Totem Circle" composed of cedar trees and carved with the names of all of the tribes encountered by Lewis and Clark's expedition on their journey west. "Artwork # 2" would feature a stone table with the Chinook creation legend inscribed on the top. "Artwork # 3" would be an amphitheater located on a mesa outcrop overlooking the small cove at Waikiki Beach and the Pacific Ocean.

An email between Lin's studio and founding director Jane Jacobsen demonstrated early concerns for the site's aesthetics: "The use of the outcrop as a destination and viewpoint can provide that 'wow' moment." (Box 6, Folder 1, Confluence Project Records, WCMss444, Whitman College and Northwest Archives) Sketches in the Whitman Archives show a path that would connect individual installations on opposite sides of the park. The realities of building on state park lands made this idea impossible. The pathway would have had to cross the main highway that runs through the park and would have required permission to build on a privately leased plot that currently houses a small convenience store and market. The language of "Totem Circle" was changed to the more culturally sensitive "Cedar Grove." The amphitheater was relocated from the mesa outcrop to the flatter land just below the hillside to account for erosion. A work as complex as the Confluence Project, located in a state park and situated on archeologically significant land, would always have to account to multiple constituencies. In addition to archeological assessments, archival records include biological surveys, environmental impact statements, correspondences with park officials at the federal and state levels, specified modifications and guidelines from the Army Corps of Engineers, and accommodations to local city and county officials, with special deference given to Chinook tribal officials. This partial list of invested parties and contributors demonstrates the scale of bureaucracy Lin and her team, and Confluence administrators were required to navigate in order to build a work of public art at this location.

The three art areas became what now resemble five distinct locations that contain discrete works of art. On the Waikiki Beachside, a bifurcated pathway sits near a parking lot and restroom. The "Amphitheater Trail," as it is identified on the Confluence website, meanders to the left as you approach from the parking lot. This walkway made from a composite of concrete and crushed oyster shell creates a shimmering effect, reminding visitors of the importance of oysters and shellfish as a food staple and a resource for the Chinook and other local Indigenous tribes of the region. The path is engraved with a Chinook praise song that was recited during the site's dedication in 2005. The text of the song includes the refrain: "We call upon the land which grows our food, the nurturing soil that sustains our lives, and we ask that it…teach us and show us the way." Native grasses were replanted, and dune restoration was completed by Greenworks, P.C., the landscaping firm contracted by Confluence. A shorter boardwalk branches off to the right from the parking lot leading down to Waikiki Beach. The planks of this pathway are engraved with the names of the tribes encountered by the Corps of Discovery expedition; those they met on the westward journey are listed on the left-hand side of the boardwalk, while those encountered during the trip back to St. Louis are written on the right-hand side. Like the Amphitheater Trail, the boardwalk is also flanked by replanted sedge and red fescue, cool-weather grasses that thrive in wet conditions.

The open-air amphitheater provides a communal gathering space. Three rows of curved wooden and concrete benches face a compact stage set atop raised piers a foot or so off the ground. A second rectangular wooden platform, approximately 4′ × 10′ sits flush with the ground in between the stage and benches. This closer platform is useful on windy days when the distance of the more scenic stage diffuses sound. The amphitheater overlooks the shoreline only a short walk away, and was the setting for both the 2005 dedication and ceremonial blessing. Since then, the stage has hosted a wide array of events and performances, including an annual concert series (held from 2005 to 2012

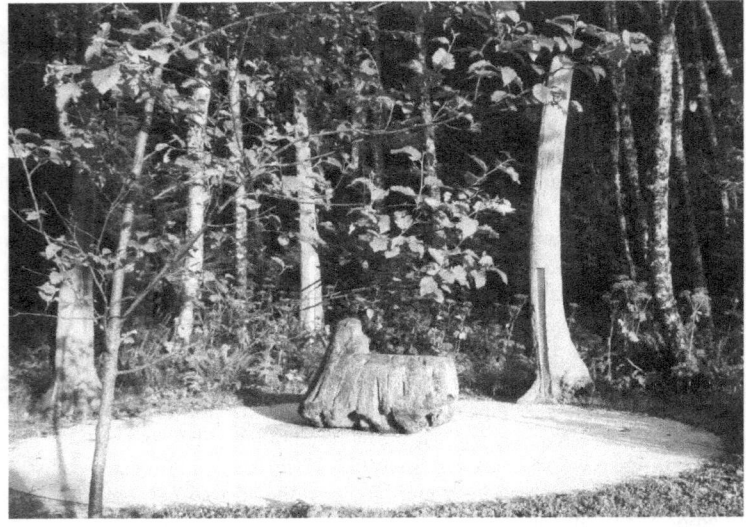

Figure 1.1 Cedar Circle at Cape Disappointment State Park with elm stump in the center surrounded by five cedar tree trunks with embedded steel supports, 2006.

Sources: Box 16, Folder 8. WCMss444. Confluence Project Records. Whitman College and Northwest Archives.

and hosted with the National Park Services), story gatherings featuring Native speakers and experts in regional history and culture, and informal meetings. While the benches provide a peaceful resting spot to look out over the cove for casual visitors, the scenic view also importantly incorporates the North Jetty. This massive infrastructural breakwater extends over a mile into the Pacific, sheltering the beach and funneling driftwood onto the shores.

Tucked behind the amphitheater is a small grove of cedar driftwood columns surrounded by old-growth forest. The Cedar Grove or Circle (formerly the Totem Circle) is composed of five dead tree trunks surrounding the stump of a dead elm that would have been alive in 1805 when the Corps of Discovery crew arrived at the ocean (Figure 1.1). Lin wrote:

> When I came to Waikiki Beach and saw the fallen logs, it was like I was seeing the history of the place in those trees. On the border between dense forest and open meadow, seven driftwood logs, half tucked into the trees, half emerging from them, invite a new look at the landscape. The trees frame the view to the landscape.
>
> (Box 3, Folder 34, "Confluence Project Records", WCMss444, Whitman College and Northwest Archives)

Like the trail, the enclosed ground is also composed of the crushed oyster shell composite. Rather than creating clear demarcations, the edges seem to merge with the surrounding forest. The trunks are anchored to the ground by matte steel support beams. Instead of concealing the beams within the trunk, they are instead a highly visible feature. Each support is roughly six to eight inches thick and centered within the trunk in such a way as to resemble a metal doorway. The effect is unavoidable. The rigid geometric plates provide a stark contrast to the organic wood of the tree trunk. The tree enframes the steel beam, the beam supports the trunk, and the trees frame the landscape. The juxtaposition of metal embedded in wood surrounding the carefully placed elm stump serves as a reminder of the Cedar Circle as a manufactured place. It is a ritualistic space, a place of performance, but of what kind? To stand in the grove and look around is to see and notice the human hand's modification of an otherwise "natural' environment. The framed landscape includes not only a view of a picturesque beach but also the edge of the amphitheater, a glimpse of the parking lot, and the enormous appendage of the North Jetty.

Across the highway at Baker Bay, Lin again worked with park staff and contractors to reclaim the small sheltered bay. In place of a series of underutilized boat docks, Lin's team planted Native trees and grasses along a short pathway that leads to an observation deck that gently curves outward into the bay. A raised metal barrier at the edge of the platform is inscribed with the short journal entry of Sergeant Patrick Gass, who described the Corps of Discovery's first glimpse of the Pacific Ocean. The path connects to a renovated boat launch and platform. Restored wetlands and riprap were used to re-grade the slope and prevent further shore erosion.

Cape Disappointment's most prominent feature is likely the columnar basalt fish scaling table placed on a refurbished outcrop overlooking Baker Bay (Figure 1.2). The table's polished top features a carved inscription of the creation myth common to the Chinook and Chehalis peoples. The story is a slightly modified version of one recorded by regional historian and ethnographer James Swan in 1857. Before humans, Too-lux (Old Man South Wind) met an old giantess (ogress) named Quoots-Hooi, during his travels north. Hungry, he asked her for some food, but she gave him a net instead and told him to catch some fish. After his fifth try, Too-lux pulled a Grampus, "or as the Indians called it, a small whale," from the water. Just as he was about to cut the fish with his knife, Quoots-Hooi warned him not to cut it crossways through the back but to split it down the middle. Ignoring her, Too-lux cut the fish the wrong way and it turned into a giant bird that took flight, blocking out the sun with its wings and shaking the earth. Thunderbird, or Hahness, as it was called, landed at a nearby mountaintop to the east, often identified as Saddleback Mountain. There, the bird laid five eggs. Some stories say Quoots-Hooi followed the bird. Others say that she found the nest while picking berries nearby. Seeing the eggs, Quoots-Hooi began "breaking and eating [them] and from these mankind were produced." When Thunderbird returned

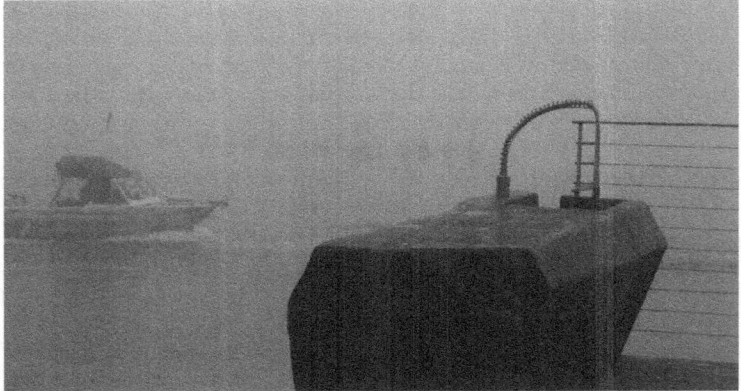

Figure 1.2 Fish cleaning table overlooking Baker Bay. The Chinook origin story text is
etched into the tabletop to the left of the spout.

Sources: Confluence *Dig*ital 2018-021-31. WCMss444. Confluence Project Records. Whitman College
and Northwest Archives.

to his nest and saw Quoots-Hooi's "mischief," he found Too-lux, and together
they searched for the ogress. Each year, Thunderbird and the South Wind
make their journey north to find Quoots-Hooi. The inscription on the tabletop
ends: "It is probably this tradition which has caused the belief that the first
salmon caught must not be cut across, but must be split down the back, and
then split in thin flakes. If it should be cut contrary to their practice, then all
the salmon will leave, and no more be taken that season." ("Thunderbird | The
Origin of the Chinook" 2017. The direct quotes are taken from the text of the
table itself. The rest of the myth is condensed for clarity from several different
sources, including Gray's own journal entry.)

The creation myth is a fitting emblem of Confluence's own agenda. The table's
orientation to a north-easterly perspective asks viewers to physically perform the
exhortation to reflect back on Lewis and Clark's journey and its aftermath. It
acknowledges the tribal histories that predate settler colonialism by millennia. It
stresses the interconnections and reliance of nature and people. People are born
of nature, and part of nature. The text is also practical in that it provides a lesson
about how to properly carve and scale a fish. Finally, it is a warning: if those sustainable rituals that allowed Indigenous peoples to thrive in this region since time
immemorial are not honored, the salmon will leave and the delicate equilibrium
between humans and nature will be damaged, perhaps permanently.

While designed as a work of art, Lin recognized the utility of the site for
local fishermen and wanted to maintain its functionality. (Box 16, Folder 4,
"Confluence Project Records", WCMss444, Whitman College and Northwest
Archives) As an earthwork, the table echoes the Minimalist sculptures from

the 1960s by Donald Judd and Robert Morris. The discourse of "earthworks" situates the Confluence Project within a broader genealogy of public art rooted in Minimalism and Conceptualism's phenomenological investigation of an artwork *in situ*. The table encourages a close textual reading while also pushing the viewer's attention outward, away from the object, toward the surrounding landscape, its development, and its history. Like those minimalist sculptures of the era to which Lin is frequently linked, the gallery and its surroundings become participants in activating the work of art. Judd's numerous untitled boxes used industrial materials and simple geometric forms to call attention to the work as part of a larger system, an ecology of the gallery or museum. Sketches and maquettes make this connection even more explicit. Visitors station themselves around the table as if it were a kind of ritual object—which, of course, it is. But the fish table was always meant to be used. Next to the inscription sits a basin with a drain and hanging faucet. During several visits to the site, I've seen people use the table to bone and clean their morning catches. Unfortunately, the table's utilitarian history is checkered. Restoration work was necessary only a few years after its dedication. It was inoperable for a period around 2010 due to environmental concerns about solid fish waste disposal and the state park's uneasiness about the degrading of the table as an art object. Box 6, Folder 17, "Confluence Project Records", WCMss444, Whitman College and Northwest Archives) It has since been restored to working order.

How Is the Confluence Project an "Environmental Work of Art"?

An environmental assessment of the Cape Disappointment site dated May 2005 in anticipation of the installations there and prepared by an outside firm serves as a template for understanding the Confluence Project's goals. "Both environmental and cultural opportunities will be provided. The environmental experience would focus on the ecological importance and significance of the riverine estuary ecosystem and ecological transition to the ocean side. The cultural history of the area, both before and after Western European arrival, would also be emphasized." (Box 6, Folder 3, "Confluence Project Records", WCMss444, Whitman College and Northwest Archives) This passage would seem to conflate the terms "environment" and "ecology," a common habit during an era only just 20 years ago when climate change was still largely an abstraction. But what do they signify now, when applied to contemporary art at a moment of planetary crisis? The last section of this chapter will briefly interrogate these terms within a larger discourse of art objects since the 1960s and introduce readers to developing theories of "eco-aesthetics" and "eco-critique" unfolding in response to Anthropogenic causes of the ongoing climate crisis. Finally, I will argue that Lin's work with the Confluence Project provides a method for confronting our current shared predicament by understanding its local, site-specific manifestations.

The term "environment" has a long association with modern and contemporary art. Wagner's Gesamkunstwerks were theatrical operatic productions that moved beyond the stage to engulf audiences in "total works of art." Kurt Schwitters Merzbau (ca. 1927–1943), the artist's home in Hanover, Germany (destroyed during World War II), featured collages and assembled objects "which quickly grew to the ceiling of his apartment…down and across the walls…up through the ceiling, down through the floor, and even out on to a small projecting roof." (Henri 1974, 18) Allan Kaprow defined "environment" as "an art form that fills an entire room (or outdoor space), surrounding the visitor and consisting of any materials whatsoever, including lights, sounds, and color." (Kaprow 1966) Although Kaprow is associated with "happenings," he differentiated between the two by insisting a happening was theatrical "in that it is performed in a given time and space." Happenings deployed the found material of everyday life but were ultimately an "extension of environments" and occurred only once and by definition could not be performed again. In the wake of the environmental movement of the 1970s, artists distanced themselves from the term, and "installation" gradually displaced the use of environment in art criticism. (Cheetham 2018, 25) Artists and critics became more attentive to how a show or exhibition was curated and to the details of the space the work occupied. (Bishop 2005) As Earthworks, Earth Art, and Land Art movements focused attention on the human impact on natural systems and the surrounding world, the environment gained greater purchase as a signifier of the natural sciences. As a result, "ecology" or "ecological" began to appear more frequently in artist statements, exhibition catalogs, and reviews.

Since the 1990s, at least, the phrase ecological art has aligned itself with climate change. Subfields and genres like "eco art," "eco-aesthetics" (in art and design), and "eco-critique" (in other humanistic modes of inquiry) are commonplace in art historical analyses as a response to the Anthropocene. This all-encompassing label for the human-produced carbon residue forever woven into the earth's geological record signaled a need for new terminology to address the scale of the threat to biological sustainability. Since Paul Crutzen and Eugene Stoermer's article published in 2000, the Anthropocene moniker has come under intense scrutiny and criticism. Feminist critics like Donna Haraway argue that the word Anthropocene reifies human exceptionalism sustains a human vs. nature binary, and "whitewashes" the causes and effects of global climate change. (Haraway 2015)

The use of ecology as an adjective in relation to creative production is equally fraught, however. Its association with scientific inquiry, colonialism, the bifurcation between Man and Nature, and the objectification of natural systems risks turning eco-into an empty signifier. I take the time to address this terminology because it is used frequently throughout this book. While the discourse of "environmental" and "ecological" artwork performs a valuable transitionary mode of understanding creative responses to the climate crisis, they are ultimately inadequate for the collective and catastrophic challenges we face in the coming years. Instead, and at the risk of oversimplification, I propose a more radical means of understanding art. We need to recognize every work of art as always already a signifier of climate change.

We are experiencing an epistemological shift that demands urgent recognition of the damage done to the environment, the ecology, the health, and habitability of the planet. We can no longer live under any illusion of a work of art as a distinct object. Work made over the last two decades at least, and from now on and until (or if) solutions are found to alleviate climate change, should be understood as part of an extractive apparatus marching us to disaster. T.J. Demos, Emily Eliza Scott, and Subhankar Banerjee write that "it is no longer possible (if it ever was) to separate nature from culture, or human from environmental systems; rather, these mutually defining conjunctions are widely recognized as the basis for the Anthropocene epoch—or the Capitalocene, as some might prefer—within which we now find ourselves." (Demos, Scott, and Banerjee 2021, 4–5) In other words, every work of art is about climate change. A more hyperbolic analogy might recognize any form of cultural production as a kind of talisman of doom, a "ruin-in-reverse" to utilize Robert Smithson's famous phrase about the infrastructural "monuments" of heavy industry doomed to dereliction in Passaic, New Jersey.

To return to the metaphor of the mirror that began this chapter and through which Lin asks viewers to understand the journey of Lewis and Clark and its aftermath, I want to return to Lippard's observation about gravel pits as inverse images of the built environment of cityscapes. While her book is mostly about the imbrications between urban and rural, the quote is a reminder to look more carefully at those so-called empty, marginal spaces—the very kinds of spaces occupied by the Confluence Project. In fact, these places were never empty or marginal and remain invaluable to the inhabitants, humans, and otherwise, who lived sustainably within them for thousands of years. They are rich in history, value, and meaning that predate the Corps of Discovery. They reflect back to us the iconography of industrialization: bridges, highways, rail systems, transmission towers, jetties, boat docks, airports, parking lots, bathrooms, riprap, and dams. Confluence recognizes and incorporates this infrastructure into the experience of art at every site and asks us, as viewers, to recognize our own imbrication within this world, forever altered by people.

References

"A Lower Columbia Chinook Historical Timeline." n.d. *PUBLIC HISTORY PDX* (blog). Accessed September 27, 2023. https://publichistorypdx.org/projects/chinook/lower-columbia-chinook-historical-timeline/

"AR6 Synthesis Report: Summary for Policymakers Headline Statements." n.d. Accessed September 27, 2023. https://www.ipcc.ch/report/ar6/syr/resources/spm-headline-statements

"Archaeology at Cathlapotle." 2016. *Chinook Story* (blog). Accessed December 17, 2016. https://chinookstory.org/archaeology-at-cathlapotle/.

Bishop, Claire. 2005. *Installation Art: A Critical History*. New York, NY: Routledge.

Cheetham, Mark A. 2018. *Landscape into Eco Art: Articulations of Nature since the '60s*. University Park, PA: The Pennsylvania State University Press.

"Confluence Project Records", WCMss444, Whitman College and Northwest Archives. https://archiveswest.orbiscascade.org/ark:/80444/xv285430

Daehnke, Jon Darin. 2017. "Chinook Resilience: Heritage and Cultural Revitalization on the Lower Columbia River." *Indigenous Confluences*. Seattle, WA: University of Washington Press.

Demos, T. J., Emily Eliza Scott, and Subhankar Banerjee. 2021. *The Routledge Companion to Contemporary Art, Visual Culture, and Climate Change*. Routledge Companions. New York, NY: Routledge, Taylor & Francis Group.

DeVoto, Bernard, ed. 1953. The Journals of Lewis and Clark. Boston, MA: Houghton Mifflin Co.

Haraway, Donna. 2015. "Anthropocene, Capitalocene, Plantationocene, Chthulucene: Making Kin." *Environmental Humanities* 6 (1): 159–65. https://doi.org/10.1215/22011919-3615934

Henri, Adrian. 1974. "Total Art: Environments, Happenings, and Performance." *The World of Art*. New York, NY: Oxford University Press.

Hunn, Eugene with James Selam and Nch'i-Wána Family. 1990. "The Big River": Mid-Columbia Indians and Their Land. Seattle, WA: University of Washington Press.

Kaprow, Allan. 1966. *Assemblage, Environments & Happenings*. New York, NY: Harry N. Abrams.

Lewis, Meriwether, Clark, William, et al. September 4, 1806 entry in The Journals of the Lewis and Clark Expedition, ed. Gary Moulton. Lincoln, NE: University of Nebraska Press / University of Nebraska-Lincoln Libraries-Electronic Text Center, 2005. http://lewisandclarkjournals.unl.edu/journals.php?id=1806-09-04.

"Thunderbird | The Origin of the Chinook." 2017. *Chinook Story* (blog). Accessed July 6, 2017. https://chinookstory.org/chinook/oral-tradition-thunderbird-origin-chinook/

2 The Land Bridge at Fort Vancouver

Maya Lin and John Paul Jones: Collaborative Tensions

The Fort Vancouver Land Bridge was perhaps the most complex site to build in an otherwise extremely complex and as-yet incomplete artistic endeavor. Maya Lin was trained as an architect and her post-memorial career is highlighted by a number of spectacular buildings and homes, including the renovation of the Neilson Library on the campus of Smith College (2021), the Museum of Chinese in America in Lower Manhattan (2009), both of which were designed in collaboration with architect William Bialosky and Partners, and the Riggio-Lynch Interfaith Chapel (2004) and the Langston Hughes Library (1999), both on the estate of author Alex Haley in Clinton, Tennessee. Because she is not a licensed architect, her building and structural designs require collaboration.

At Fort Vancouver, Lin worked with Native American architect Johnpaul Jones (Cherokee-Choctaw) of Jones & Jones, a Seattle-based firm known for their thoughtful integration of landscape and nature into the built environment. Most famously, Jones was a principal architect in charge of landscape for the National Museum of the American Indian, a branch of the Smithsonian situated on the National Mall in Washington, DC. Jones & Jones also completed the Southern Ute Cultural Center (2011) in Ignacio, Colorado, the University of Washington Intellectual House (2014), a dedicated gathering space for Native American students, staff, and faculty, and arboreal habitats for animals at the Dublin Zoo in Ireland (2016). While Lin's input and expertise helped shape the end result, it is important to note that since the Land Bridge's dedication in 2008, and a rededication in 2022, Lin is no longer listed as the primary designer. In fact, Lin has removed the Vancouver installation from her website entirely. Likewise, the Jones & Jones site does not mention Lin at all in the didactic text that accompanies images of the Land Bridge. (The Confluence Project website states: "The Land Bridge was designed by architect Johnpaul Jones with consultation from Maya Lin.") Instead, while Lin is currently referred to as a "consultant" on the project, Jones & Jones are now given sole credit for the completed structure in the literature and publicity about the Confluence Project.[1] This issue raises thorny questions about authorial intent and artistic collaboration, which are not

DOI: 10.4324/9781003309024-3

easily resolved. What was the extent of Lin's input at the different stages of the Fort Vancouver site project? What was the extent of Jones & Jones's contribution if Lin no longer considers this "her work"? Finally, how might this shift away from Lin as the primary artistic voice alter our understanding of the Confluence Project as a work of art with a single, unique vision? The desire to understand a work of art as the product of an individual authorial voice is one of the most stubborn myths of Western cultural production. It should be demystified, especially when discussing large-scale, fabricated, public projects that require the expertise of multiple, often competing voices, as this chapter will make clear throughout.

The City of Vancouver and the National Parks Service, which owns and operates the buildings and grounds at the historic site, had long advocated for enhancements to Fort Vancouver, including improved pedestrian access to the nearby Columbia River. The park is a 209-acre peninsula ascending northward from the banks of the Columbia River into surrounding residential neighborhoods Figure 2.1. The eastern edge is bounded by Interstate 5, one of the busiest commercial thoroughfares in the country. Pearson Air Field, a small municipally owned airport, and the Pearson Air Museum sit at the western edge. At the southern edge, in between the River and park lie the Burlington-Northern Santa Fe (BNSF) Railroad and Highway 14, a four-lane state highway that connects the City of Vancouver with nearby Portland. Fort Vancouver was established on a historical floodplain of the Columbia River.

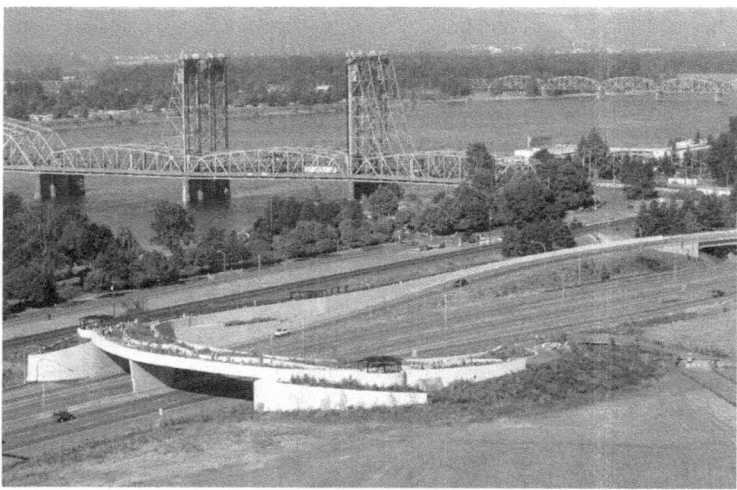

Figure 2.1 Aerial view of the Land Bridge at Fort Vancouver, ca. 2008. The bridge spans Highway 14 in Vancouver, Washington. In the background are railroad tracks, truss bridge, and warehouses along the Columbia River waterfront.

Source: Confluence Digital 2018-028-007. WCMss444. Confluence Project Records. Whitman College and Northwest Archives.

Its proximity to the river is its defining feature and the reason for the historical importance of this site dating well before Euro-American colonization.

For centuries, this spot was used by Native Americans as an important access point between the Columbia and the high plains of Central Washington. Confluence Project promotional materials consistently state that the bridge restores "the ancient crossroads of the Klickitat Trail and the Columbia River." (Box 4, Folder 38, "Confluence Project Records", WCMss444, Whitman College and Northwest Archives) For decades, pedestrian access between the Fort and the River was cut off by the highway and railroad tracks. The symbolic value of reconnecting the River, Fort, and trailhead was a primary reason for choosing this location as a Confluence site. I take the time to detail this modern infrastructure in and around Fort Vancouver National Park—highways, train tracks, airports, and runways—because the design of each Confluence installation and site is, I argue, not intended to hide or shield the industrial development of the Columbia from the view of visitors. It is a deliberate incorporation of the contemporary landscape alongside the historic buildings and grounds of the old Fort. This is not to say that to visit the Land Bridge is an unpleasant experience. The setting contains inviting green spaces in the spring and early summer. The Bridge itself combines an outdoor natural historical museological experience with trails and pathways more common to grand civic parks. As this chapter will demonstrate, the design of the bridge is intentional in making these surroundings a part of the overall experience. This is not only a confluence of river systems and waterways but also an attempt to merge the various temporal dimensions of the Indigenous, precontact settler colonial era, the Fort's pivotal role in the broader development of the region, and the contemporary reality of the fossil-dependent, carbon-emitting present. If the historical experience of the Fort and the Land Bridge's accompanying displays create a diachronic representation of space and place, the installation also asks viewers to see, hear, and smell the synchronic features contributing to the climate crisis.

Before the Fort: A History of Place

Written historical records about this area typically begin with Lewis and Clark, focus on the importance of the Fort in the development of Vancouver, the River and its tributaries, and end in the present. If the construction of Fort Vancouver on the north side of the Columbia near the mouth of the Willamette in 1824 is so frequently referenced in published scholarship about the history of this site, it is because of the failure of Western scholarship to account for, or even acknowledge, the thousands of years in which this region was inhabited by Indigenous peoples prior to Euro-American contact and settlement. This is also a failure of imagination.

The area around what is now Vancouver sits at the juncture of the Columbia and one of its largest tributaries, the Willamette River, which runs parallel to the western tier of the Cascades throughout much of Oregon. Geography, climate, and topography made this a vital point of contact between the Salish-speaking tribes—predominantly Chinook and Cowlitz, and Sahaptin-speaking tribes—Klickitat, Yakama, Walla Walla, Umatilla, and Nez Perce, to name only several. Where the park is now was once a series of floodplains that fed nearby prairies and forests. Native peoples, usually women, cultivated and harvested abundant balsam root, huckleberries, camas lily, and wapato, using these crops for food, medicine, and baskets. The area was known to Indians as "skit-so-to-ho" by the Chinook, "ala-sikas" ("the place of the mud turtles") by the Klickitat, and "alasikas," or "place of turtles" by the Sahaptin. (National Park Service 2002, 28. Box 10, Folder 12)

For centuries, this was the terminus of the Klickitat Trail, which linked the tribes of the prairies to those of the river and coast. The site was a vital trade nexus that formed one of the "Great Markets" of the West. Smelt, sturgeon, salmon, and wapato were exchanged for resources of camas, oak, berries, and game animals. (National Park Service 2002, 28) Coniferous forests and the advanced building skills of river and coastal tribes combined to create a robust culture of the canoe. Here and at other marketplaces along the Columbia, there also existed an active trade in slaves, horses, and European goods predating explorer contact. Settler, explorer, and travel journals all note that slavery was practiced by many tribes, but the Chinook were well known for using captive peoples from nearby tribes or raiding parties from the south as laborers. Gabriel Franchère, a French clerk who signed on to John Jacob Astor's fur enterprise in Astoria, observed the practice firsthand: "They procure their slaves from neighboring tribes and from the interior in exchange for beads and furs. They treat them with humanity while their services are useful, but as soon as they become incapable of labor, neglect them and suffer them to perish of want." (Hunt 1918, 280. Hunt's article is characterized by inaccuracy and bias but the historiography of settler accounts of slavery in the Pacific Northwest is significant.)

Alexander Ross, a Scottish clerk for the Pacific Fur Company, wrote that the Chinookan people "are a commercial rather than a warlike people. Traffic in slaves and furs is their occupation." (Ross 1904, 87–88) If the practice of slavery by Native Americans is a surprise to contemporary readers, it should serve as a caution against the romanticization of Indian life that can be its own representational burden. Like their use of fire to alter their environment, an image of Indigenous peoples as beneficent caretakers of the land, victims and martyrs of colonial violence, or spiritual healers is always much more complicated than the lived experiences of human beings, no matter the setting, time, or place. To perpetuate these myths risks dehumanizing Native Americans in the same manner as the historical stereotypes of uncivilized savages. It should also serve as a reminder of the commonplace of slavery in the newly established United States, a fact reinforced by the presence of York, Capt. Clark's enslaved servant and a crucial member of the Corps of Discovery crew, who was denied his freedom by Clark when they returned to St. Louis. (Parks 2018) The slavery practiced by Indians, while still abhorrent to contemporary ideals, should also not be confused with the chattel slavery of Africans brought to the American colonies and nascent United States and practiced in the American South.

Upon arrival near the Willamette River, the crew immediately recognized the appeal of this neck of the river. They found hunting easy and game plentiful. There were villages with timber "cabbens" built with split boards or thatched with straw. John Ordway, a member of the expedition, noted: "the natives verry numerous, the country appears good, the Soil rich." Sergeant Patrick Gass commented on the "handsome islands" (Sauvie and Hayden) and called this a "beautiful part of the river." Private Joseph Whitehouse likewise claimed that "The Indians appear'd to be very numerous, The Country pleasant, the Soil rich & Game tolerably plenty." (Lewis, et al., November 6, 1805 entry in The Journals of the Lewis and Clark Expedition 2005) On the return trip, Lewis found the valley a highly desirable place for future (White) settlements and estimated the region could accommodate up to 50,000 people "if properly cultivated." (Lewis, et al., March 30, 1806 entry in The Journals of the Lewis and Clark Expedition 2005)

They also encountered a land that was carefully managed and cultivated, complicating long-held stereotypes about the untouched wilderness and pristine landscapes that drew settlers to the West. A Story Gathering public talk hosted by Confluence in February 2020 addressed many of the misconceptions about the inland Pacific Northwest and Native American practices of agriculture and cultivation of the landscape that predate colonization. Mike Iyall, historian and member of the Cowlitz Indian Tribe, began the event by referencing the practice of using controlled burns to create and manage large swaths of prairie: "The early explorers thought they were seeing an untouched ground. No! They were seeing a maintained environment." ("Confluence Podcast: Vancouver Story Gathering" 2020) Iyall cites Robert Boyd's *Indians, Fire, and the Land in the Pacific Northwest*, which combined research from the fields of archeology, paleobotany, and ethnography to argue that Native Americans actively altered their surroundings to create or enhance physical conditions to their benefit. (Boyd 1999) This evidence also undermines the myth that Indian land was a mismanaged resource—an enormous justification for appropriating and dispossessing Native Americans from ceded territory during the reservation era. This actively maintained region was home to an abundance of peoples for thousands of years prior to settler contact.

Even before Lewis and Clark's arrival, the Indian population was devastated by smallpox, influenza, and "ague." The Corps of Discovery journal entries west of the Cascades frequently mention signs of Indians afflicted by smallpox or measles. When the Hudson's Bay Company (HBC) moved its headquarters from Astoria to Fort Vancouver in 1824, this beautiful part of the river became an even more deadly disease vector. Native populations had already been reduced by as much as half by the time of Lewis and Clark's arrival, and some estimates suggest that an additional 90 percent of the Indigenous population of the territory was killed during a four-year outbreak between 1830 and 1833. As Hunn notes, mass mortality was perceived as a sign from God to settlers and missionaries, further fueling the religious foundations of Manifest Destiny. (Hunn 1990, 31)

The fur trade fueled intense competition in the Pacific Northwest between British, French, and American interests. John Jacob Astor abandoned Fort Astoria to the British and the HBC. In 1821, the Crown forced a merger between the North West Company and the HBC and established the Columbia Department. The newly merged entity relocated its regional headquarters further inland on the Columbia near the mouth of the Willamette. As noted, this location was highly desirable and well-trafficked. Chief Factor John McLoughlin oversaw construction of a sawmill, dairy, tannery, and gristmill and expanded the company's trade interests to include timber, beef, and grain. A large village rapidly developed alongside the Fort and was, for a time, one of the largest settlements in the West. The population spike and broadening commercial interests quickly attracted a diverse population of settlers, laborers, and trappers. The village was dubbed "Kanaka" because of its large population of Hawaiians who were recruited for their skills in canoe building and navigation. The fur companies had long (unofficially) encouraged intermarriage between their employees and Indians. "Blanket marriages," also known as "marriage à la façon du pays" were a way of easing trade disputes and forming alliances among disparate communities and was widely practiced at Kanaka and throughout the territory. As conflict between Indians and settlers increased over the first half of the nineteenth century, the Fort was increasingly used as a base from which to launch violent attacks. It also became a notorious stockade for captured warriors, and later an internment camp for larger tribal groups in preparation for relocation to reservations. (Deur 2012, 185)

Indian displacement began in the late eighteenth century and accelerated with the passage of Andrew Jackson's Indian Removal Act in 1830, which relocated tribes West of the Mississippi in what is now known as the Trail of Tears. In the Great Plains and Northwest, the process began less than two decades later. In 1846, Great Britain agreed to forfeit its claims to the territory when it signed the Oregon Treaty and the HBC began to divest from its holdings. By then, the Oregon Trail was firmly established as a migrant settler corridor to the West with Fort Vancouver serving as a destination of choice. Following the treaty councils of 1848–1855 that set the initial reservation boundaries in Oregon and Washington, the federal government reneged on its promises and broke its contracts. The discovery of gold on the Yakama Reservation and in Idaho attracted fortune seekers and miners with even less regard for territorial boundaries and led to violent conflicts throughout the Plateau. The conclusion of the Yakima War in 1858 resulted in the relocation of "Vancouver Indians" to nearby reservations, including the Yakama, Grand Ronde, and Warm Springs. (Deur 2012, 169–70) Native peoples were often dispersed regardless of tribal affiliation and reservation territories were further carved away over the next 30 years. Many Chinook, Cowlitz, and Klickitat were isolated from their traditional homelands or forced into uneasy alliances with once-hostile neighbors.

Oregon was granted statehood in 1859. A provision barring Black people from owning property or making contracts was written into the state constitution, even though Oregon was technically an anti-slavery state that fought for the Union during the Civil War. Washington would have to wait another three decades before President Harrison would sign the bill making it the 42nd state. (Its constitution contained no such exclusionary clauses, although racial covenants would become common on property deeds throughout the state until banned by the Supreme Court in 1948.) During this period, the area around Vancouver continued to develop as a vital port connecting inland industries to global markets via the Pacific Ocean. Wheat, timber, salmon, and, following large-scale irrigation projects, fruit orchards were the primary commercial exports. Steamships transported goods and people along the Columbia until the railroads finally connected the Eastern continent with the resource-rich West. An airfield was built at Fort Vancouver, now called the Vancouver Barracks, for the centennial celebration of the Lewis and Clark expedition in 1905, and during World War I, a massive spruce mill was built almost overnight to supply war efforts and just as quickly vanished after the fighting ceased in Europe.

The era of dam building for hydropower began during the Great Depression with the construction of the Bonneville and Grand Coulee stations. The sustained control of river water facilitated the expansion of extractive industries. The Aluminum Company of America (ALCOA) built its first smelter in 1939, and the Reynolds (no relation) Metals Company built its own facility at Longview, Washington, a year later. With the outbreak of World War II, Kaiser Shipyards constructed a major production facility for troop transport vessels and aircraft carriers in Vancouver. The Kaiser factory alone was responsible for a huge demographic shift in the Portland-Vancouver area. The company actively recruited a large African-American labor pool from the South. The city of Vanport was built to house an estimated 100,000 workers, approximately 15,000 of whom were Black and who were beset by Jim Crow-style racism and segregation, a legacy of Oregon's exclusionary laws. (Maben 1987) The three regional Kaiser shipyards also attracted thousands of Native Americans who left their reservations to work in defense industries. (Lansing 2003) After the War, aluminum production continued to expand throughout the region and along the major waterways. The number of smelters grew to ten by the 1960s and, at one point in time, accounted for 40 percent of the entire national output and 6–7 percent of the world's supply of aluminum (Northwest Power and Conservation Council 2023).

In just one century, the Columbia River was irrevocably transformed in ways that would be inconceivable to the people who lived through the ten millennia that preceded it. The infrastructure required for the industrial development of the region necessitated dams, dredging, and rerouting of tributaries, in addition to the ancillary facilities—factories, warehouses, highways, and ports—needed to support the transportation of goods, people, and services. Whole cities appeared in such rapid succession as like a montage from a classic educational cartoon illustrating the phenomenon of urbanization and "progress." With it all came toxic contaminants such as cyanide, fluoride, petroleum hydrocarbons, poly-chlorinated biphenyls (PCBs), trichloroethylene (TCE), heavy metals, waste-piles, tailings, runoff, and numerous other lethal byproducts that have poisoned the river water and the soil, killed off salmon and other fish species, and brought them to the brink of extinction. (Fisheries 2022) This dialectic dance of death, the interminable feedback loop between industrial progress and environmental degradation, is where we are now trapped and from which the window of escape is rapidly closing. For now, I close this section with a quote from Jane Jacobsen from a Confluence Project newsletter dated Spring 2004 in anticipation of the dedication of the Land Bridge:

> More than 50 million tons of goods are shipped on the Columbia each year—everything from wheat and corn to petroleum and forest products uniting rural and urban areas of the Northwest in commerce, and connect-ing the region with global markets as well... Just as it was a center of life for thousands of years and one of the Corps of Discovery's primary destinations, the Columbia continues to be the great river of the west. Our responsibility is to keep it so. Our goal is to instill in [Confluence] visitors the same respect and love we have for the river while reexamining our relationship with this unique natural resource and the life it sustains.
> (Box 3, Folder 34, "Confluence Project Records", WCMss444, Whitman College and Northwest Archives)

Perhaps no statement is more emblematic of the ambivalent position that char-acterizes much of the Confluence Project. It is at once an effort to honor a moment in which an era of Anthropogenic climate change can be said to have begun and a plea to reinvent and reimagine a more sustainable relationship with our shared environment.

The Art of the Vancouver Land Bridge

In the Confluence Project archives held at Whitman College, an undated map showing the outline of the park with Highway 14 running alongside it serves to illustrate earlier plans for a bridge at the site and how the evolution of those plans would ultimately realize something far more unique. On this map, two short, hand-drawn parallel lines indicating a pedestrian bridge connect a stairway on the Fort side with another approximately 100 feet away to the Old Apple Tree Orchard on the highway's riverside. Someone—perhaps a park employee or city engineer—created a quick, pragmatic, provisional solution: the shortest distance between two points is always a straight line. The undated map appears in a folder with documents from the early 1990s. Later planning documents render a more fully realized drawing of a much more ambitiously designed pedestrian bridge complete with trees and shrubs and now identified as a "land bridge" and dated 2004. (Box 16, Folder 25, "Confluence Project Records", WCMss444, Whitman College and Northwest Archives)

What happened in the meantime to so drastically alter the experience of the location, elevating the structure from a piece of utilitarian infrastructure to an art environment? One way to think about the two radically different designs can be understood through Linda Tuhiwai-Smith's assessment of the "spatial vocabulary of colonialism." She argues that colonial strategies that include mapping, the platting of towns, and Western architectural practices are predicated on three elements: the line, the center, and the outside.

> The 'line' is important because it was used to map territory, to survey land, to establish boundaries and to mark the limits of colonial power. The 'centre' is important because orientation to the centre was an orientation to the system of power. The 'outside' is important because it positioned territory and people in an oppositional relation to the colonial centre.
>
> (Smith 2012, 55)

The Land Bridge at Fort Vancouver disrupts the Euclidean geometry of the Euro-American empirical design program. In addition to the "no frills" bridge that was planned prior to Lin and Jones's involvement, an early proposal for a "Great Circle Bridge" was also considered. While conceptually compelling, it proved both difficult to realize and cost prohibitive. A third option was the terraced land bridge that was eventually built. Public meetings were held and several regional publications covered the deliberations and progress of the design. An early "Frequently Asked Questions" document was circulated internally during these occasions and used to promote the Fort Vancouver proposal. It would "endow communities along the Columbia River with permanent artworks; empower people of all ages to explore history, engage in civic dialogue about critical issues, and envision the future; contribute to the preservation of our shared natural resources [and] cultural traditions; promote sustainable growth for local economies in the lower Columbia River Basin by creating a significant heritage tourism corridor." (Box 10, Folder 1, "Confluence Project Records", WCMss444, Whitman College and Northwest Archives) This is the first time such language appears in Confluence archival materials. It indicates an organization still workshopping a cohesive message meant for a broad audience. These goals might also be interpreted as a justification for the bridge's high cost. In 2004, the year when construction was scheduled to begin, the budget estimate for the Land Bridge was $8.7 million. In 2005, that estimate was raised to $10.8 million and was adjusted again the following year to $12.5 million. (Box 10, Folder 7, "Confluence Project Records", WCMss444, Whitman College and Northwest Archives) Of this, approximately two-thirds of the cost came from federal and state agencies. The rest was raised through private donors (Figure 2.2).

The resulting structure is an elegant, sweeping pedestrian walkway and interpretive trail that connects the historic Fort Vancouver National Park with the banks of the Columbia River. It is an earthen and concrete overpass that hosts a teeming array of plant-life. The trail is approximately a half-mile long,

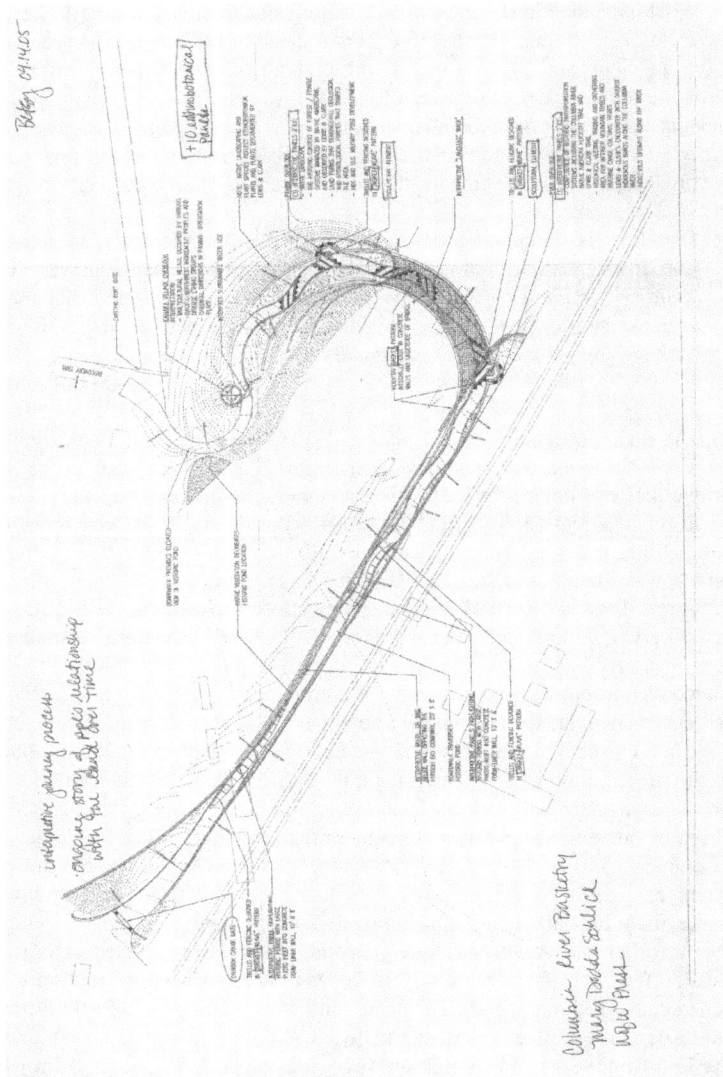

Figure 2.2 Design drawing of Land Bridge plan by Jones & Jones Architects and Land-scape Architects featuring handwritten notes and call-outs for important thematic elements such as the "interpretive journey," overlooks, reintroduction of ethnobotanical plantings, language walk, mural wall, and "canoe Gate," later renamed "Welcome Gate." 2005. Dated April 14, 2005.

Sources: Box 10, Folder 15. WCMss444_010_015_001. Confluence Project Records. Whitman College and Northwest Archives.

from the path's edge at the national park to the historic Apple Tree Grove on the opposite side. The span of the bridge over Highway 14 is 40 feet wide and roughly 200 yards between the two overlooks that bookend the structure. The middle section arcs southward in a crescent moon-like shape over the highway. Over that length, the trail winds and meanders, creating opportunities to pause, read, rest, look, learn, and reflect. An article published in *Landscape Architecture* just prior to the bridge's 2008 dedication explained the complexity of the design and its construction:

> Engineering the Land Bridge was a special challenge. The bridge features 15 totally different retaining wall designs, including soil-nailed and mechanically stabilized earth (all faced with concrete) along with traditional cast-in-place and cantilevered walls. No radius is the same, and no one had to bend more than the state highway engineers, who had never before faced an overpass with lateral curves.
>
> (Enlow 2009, 6)

The article also discusses the difficulty of building a bridge near a small craft airport. Lin and Jones wanted to maintain 360-degree views of the surroundings, including river, highway, interchange, trains, bridges, and park. An overlook that would not only allow for all of these sights but also not interfere with planes landing or taking off required negotiations with the Federal Aviation Administration. (Enlow 2009, 6) The trail, including bridge, consists of six distinct regions: three themed overlooks, a language walk, a timeline path featuring photographic murals depicting different stages of development in and around the Fort, and a Welcome Gate, a large sculptural frame at the riverside entry to the bridge designed by artist Lillian Pitt. Although this interpretation can sound programmatic, the experience of visiting the bridge embraces the decolonial rejection of line, center, and outside discussed by Tuhiwai-Smith.

The following description's orientation is from east to west, beginning at the Fort and ending with Pitt's Welcome Gate. The path to the bridge leads visitors through a tight circular pattern with a slight graded incline. (The bridge is ADA compliant and appropriate for visitors in most any physical condition.) The walkway then veers sharply to the left, taking visitors alongside an embankment and the highway. The sound of speeding cars is unavoidable at nearly all times of day or night and the landscaping between the path and highway is minimal until the first overlook. The juxtaposition of traffic noise to the right with the grassy fields and historic structures of the Fort to the left can be jarring. Mounted placards begin to identify Indigenous plants. The first overlook appears a few yards ahead on the left-hand side, which Confluence identifies as the "Village Overlook." Through a clearing of trees, a view of the site of Kanaka Village and the original footprint of the HBC can be seen. The overlook is an open circular platform approximately 12 feet in diameter and features six squat crenellated benches, on which are affixed steel plates identifying the "People" referring to the Indigenous inhabitants of the site with whom Lewis and Clark made contact and prior to colonial settlement. The plates are attached to both the inside and outside of the circle and etched with Chinookin, Sahaptin, and Anglicized names of the regional tribes. For example, "Tannama" is carved in large letters on one of the plates. Underneath, in smaller text, is carved "Umatilla." "Tananma" is the term for "our people" in Sahaptin dialect spoken by members of the Confederated Tribes of the Umatilla Indian Reservation in Pendleton, Oregon. Confluence consulted with members of each of the represented tribes.

At the center of the overlook is a small feature often neglected by visitors. Its value, however, is becoming increasingly important in an era of catastrophic droughts and wildfires like those experienced statewide in 2020 and 2022. A small, circular wrought iron drain sits at the center of the platform. The drainage vents resemble the ridges of a chambered nautilus, a reminder of the Columbia's connection to the ocean and the artwork at Cape Disappointment. Text stating "Water Collection for Landbridge Landscape" is engraved along the outer edge like the writing on an ordinary manhole plate. The drain is part of a larger storage and irrigation system. Here, water is channeled along the pedestrian paths into a graded trench, emptied into a holding cistern, and recirculated via a pumping system as needed. This feature models a sustainable relationship to the Columbia River and provides opportunities for education and preservation of the riparian landscape. (Box 10, Folder 25, "Confluence Project Records", WCMss444, Whitman College and Northwest Archives)

The walkway then weaves away from the highway curving back toward the Fort and gradually ascends for another 100 feet to the second overlook. Along the way, visitors pass terraced landscapes of native flora on opposite sides. The highway side includes chokecherry, ocean spray, and snowberry to "give a sense of the grassland" and white oak trees. The landscape facing the fort is dotted with native grasses, serviceberry, nootka rose, and wildflowers to "represent a dry prairie native ecosystem." ("Vancouver Land Bridge Art" n.d.) The second overlook is situated near the point where the bridge starts to traverse the highway and provides a view of these diverse ecologies. The "Prairie Overlook" is stationed at a slightly higher elevation, a point at which you can look back down the path from which you came, out over the grasslands of the National Park, or in a westerly direction to the other side of the bridge and the third overlook, the "River Overlook."

The Prairie Overlook encourages visitors to gain a multisensory experience of the site by using artwork, architecture, and didactic placards within the semicircular enclosure. Steel panels are attached at waist-level around the perimeter on which are carved "Land" in nine native languages, including Chinookan, Sahaptin, and Nez Perce. Mounted text panels atop the barrier include descriptions of Mt. Hood (visible to the south on a clear day), the prairie landscape and replantings, and a summary of the site's long history as a gathering place predating settler contact. The Prairie Overlook, while sharing some of the features of the Village circle, adds a new element—an eight-foot-tall, open-air, steel canopy. Its unique geometric design is a series of interlocking circles anchored by five support bars anchored to the walls of the circular platform supporting its cantilevered roof. If viewed from directly below or above, as is possible for those taking off or landing at Pearson Air Field, the small aircraft strip at the south end of the National Park grounds, the canopy might resemble a net or the underside of a woven flat-bottom basket. Tribal design patterns are repeated in relief along the circular wall and in colored brick pavers on the pathway. In the center of the circle sit rounded benches that curve inward and arranged to evoke basketry patterns characteristic of Lower Columbia River tribes. Artist Lillian Pitt played an active role in designing this feature, including polished steel panels that surround the inner circle with carved cutouts resembling the ancient petroglyphs of the Columbia River Gorge.

At the opposite end of the bridge is the River Overlook. The platform is similar in look and design to the Prairie Overlook. It features a nearly identical canopy, central bench with petroglyph-inspired carve-outs, basketry patterns in the walls and walkway, and engraved steel panels that list the different tribal names for "River." For example, "Nch'i-Wána" is the term used for "Big River" by both the Yakama and Umatilla Indian nations. The River Overlook is situated at the highest point of the trail, offering a panoramic view of the Columbia. It is also mere feet away from the busy freight rail tracks. This station, like the others before it, choreographs a multisensory experience that asks viewers to acknowledge, see, hear, and smell this complex intersection of culture, commerce, and history. Reading the panels and placards along the overlook's rim means walking its perimeter. To look at the art is also to encounter its context: the traffic patterns of the highway below, the industrial architecture of the riverside, boxy container cars or railroad tankers speeding by, pedestrians walking or biking over the bridge. For those who choose to engage with it, the art of the Land Bridge provides a temporal disorientation. Petroglyphs and historical photographs blend with contemporary technologies of the fossil fuel-based economy. Indigenous plants and text are juxtaposed with the urban skylines of Vancouver and Portland. Jets landing or taking off from nearby Portland International Airport dwarf the smaller planes utilizing the runway warning lights of Pearson Air Field. Timber barges and smaller fishing boats cruise along in the distance. The Land Bridge's incorporation of its surroundings alongside the artwork is a matter-of-fact acknowledgment of the natural and human forces that have brought us to a moment of uncertainty about our shared futures and call into question modernity's progress.

From the River Overlook to the Welcome Gate, the interpretive trail extends in a straight northeasterly direction for another 500–600 feet, sandwiched by the train tracks and the highway. Landscape infill and a retaining wall shield pedestrians from some of the noise and partially obstruct the views of the surroundings. Plantings include dogwood, red alder, vine maple trees, and ferns. At the point where the ramp descends toward the riverside, "forest plantings shift to a native wet prairie of lupines, sedges, meadow rushes and camas lily." ("Vancouver Land Bridge Art" n.d.) An iron railing in the shape of irregularly sized sticks or short tree branches runs along the riverside barrier. The wall also provides a background for six mounted photographic reproductions showing the Fort and its surrounding area from different historical periods and interspersed every few yards. The titles are etched in relief above the images. A black-and-white photograph of an aircraft carrier being launched from the Kaiser Shipyards during World War II is followed by an earlier panoramic photo of the spruce mill in operation at the site during World War I. The next two panels are images of the U.S. Military Post; the first is a photograph circa 1860. The second is a birds-eye lithograph of Hudson Bay Company showing the historic fort, exterior walls, the prefecture's house, cultivated agricultural fields, and a wagon train arriving with goods. The last image is a famous watercolor by nineteenth-century artist Paul Kane entitled, A Chinook Traveling Lodge, with a view of Mt. Hood. (1846–1847, Stark Museum of Art, Orange, Texas) The image features Chinook dwellings sheltered by trees in the foreground and middle ground, and a view of the Willamette River looking south toward the Cascade peak.

The inclusion of these images along the interpretive trail was a source of controversy at the time of the Land Bridge's dedication in 2008. A close reading of the Vancouver Land Bridge site, alongside a discussion of the opening ceremony led Daehnke to argue that the iconographical project of the photomurals presents "a fairly overt message of American progress and Manifest Destiny." (Daehnke 2018, 511) He also notes that the opening ceremony, which included the Pledge of Allegiance, the singing of America the Beautiful, attendance by city and state government officials, and a performance by a Scottish-American bagpipe band "muted" the Native American presence and history. For Daehnke, the imagery and dedication amount to a whitewashing of history: … rather than transforming and reimagining the story of Lewis and Clark, [these factors] serve to further assimilate the Native American story as one more component of the American master narrative." For him, the images and initial performances "create a false equation of Indigenous and settler experiences on the landscape, distance and erase the tragedies of colonialism, and perpetuate stereotypes of nonanthropogenic landscapes (Daehnke 2018, 504).

This interpretation is compelling but less attentive to the symbolic importance of the Welcome Gate designed by prominent Northwest artist Lillian Pitt. Her Native heritage (Warm Springs, Yakama, and Wasco), the materials, and thematic motifs of the Gate mark an unavoidable, visually striking Indian presence at the trail's beginning or ending. Two hand-carved wooden canoe paddles sit atop two stripped Port Orford cedar trunk posts. The posts are surrounded by smaller volcanic columnar basalt pillars on which Pitt repeats the petroglyphic motifs found elsewhere on the structure. Basalt deposits and formations are visible throughout the Columbia River Gorge and a material used frequently at other Confluence sites, such as Cape Disappointment and Sacajawea State Park. Two 30-inch cast glass masks are embedded into the canoe blades on opposite sides. Pitt's use of light, opaque glass and the positioning of the masks directly opposite one another can make it appear as if the artist used one sculptural element, a block of glass with a double-sided face. But the slight tilt of the paddles toward the ground makes this a trick of the eye. They are, in fact, separate pieces. These faces watch visitors coming or going (Figure 2.3).

Pitt is widely known for her masks and her work often freely adapts the famous petroglyph visage known as Tsagiglalal, a Wishram word loosely translated as "She who watches all who are coming and going." (McClure 1978) Tsagiglalal/She Who Watches is a sacred image located in what is now

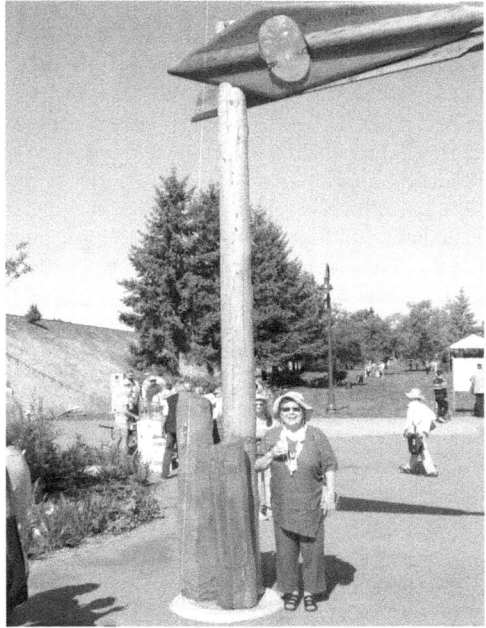

Figure 2.3 Artist Lillian Pitt (Wasco, Yakama) stands beneath her design for the Welcome Gate on the southwest side of the Land Bridge, 2008.

Sources: Confluence Digital 2018-028-023. WCMss444. Confluence Project Records. Whitman College and Northwest Archives.

Columbia Hills State Park, a few miles from the banks of the Columbia between The Dalles and Celilo Village. Its date of origin is unknown, but comparison with other nearby petroglyphs and pictographs mean it predates the Oregon Trail, the remnants of which can be seen across the river. Its location near the proximity of the Klikitat Trail is another symbolic connection between the upriver Plateau peoples and those of the Lower Columbia, enhancing the importance of the Fort Vancouver area and the value of the Land Bridge as a restorative artery for community, trade, and exchange. The ancient image is often described as the head of an anthropomorphic animal, usually a bear, or even an owl. In tribal mythologies, Tsagiglalal was a benevolent woman chief, a leader of all who lived in the region "before Coyote came up the river and changed things, and people were not yet real people." (Ramsey 1977, 53) Coyote told her that the world would soon change and that women would no longer be allowed to be chiefs. He changed her into a rock and commanded her to "watch over the people who live at this place ..." (Ibid.) Since time immemorial, Native peoples have recognized the all-seeing power of Tsagiglalal.

While a standalone artwork not involving Lin had been planned after approval of the Land Bridge design, the Welcome Gate (or "canoe gate" as it was initially called) was a competitive commission won by Pitt. (Box 10, Folder 15, "Confluence Project Records", WCMss444, Whitman College and Northwest Archives) Her early sketches for her proposal more closely resemble Tsagiglalal. The final result, while sharing some of the features of She Who Watches, appears more human in form. A rounded, oblong head with similar spiral-like shapes forming the brow and eyes is clearly inspired by Tsagiglalal. Gold-plated insets resembling arrowheads descend downward from the forehead and across both cheeks. In her proposal, Pitt calls these masks a "Chinook woman." "Filling with natural light, the mask of the Chinook woman will glow and welcome all those who come and go. I prefer the clear color because it gives a strong spiritual grounded feeling." (Box 9, Folder 27, "Confluence Project Records", WCMss444, Whitman College and Northwest Archives) Pitt is also credited with the pictograph-style designs found in the Village and River Overlooks and has regularly contributed to Confluence Project events and programs, including Stories from Our Ancestors and Confluence in the Classroom and a design proposal for a smaller, complimentary installation at the unbuilt Celilo Falls location.

Pitt's use of the Tsagiglalal/She Who Watches motif symbolically reclaims and reframes the site through Native eyes. The artist is explicit about the importance of the figure's gender, a representation of the role of women as leaders and negotiators for much of the river trade. It serves as a reminder of ways of living that exist outside of Western patriarchal systems. A review of Pitt's work at an exhibition at the Warm Springs Museum in 2000 that appeared in *Art in America* remarked on the importance of Tsagiglalal in Pitt's work, noting that the watchful figure "encourages good behavior and an awareness of one's environment ... Pitt presents a delicate plea for responsible conduct toward the environment as ecological issues are hotly debated in the Northwest." (Taylor 2000, 139)

Like the design of the Bridge itself, the Welcome Gate's deployment of ancient petroglyphs along the Bridge provides an additional opportunity to reframe Daehnke's arguments about how the site foregrounds the settler colonial and industrial history of the location at the expense of Native histories and experiences. There is no doubt that a work of art commemorating Lewis and Clark's westward journey and Vancouver's history as a military outpost and site of wartime manufacture connotes the region's association with American imperialist ambitions. That the Land Bridge simultaneously doubles as a piece of functioning infrastructure for tourists and residents is in itself a statement about the inordinate value our society has placed on the unfettered movement of goods, services, and commerce often at the expense of the health and welfare of our shared ecology. Pitt's comparatively small gesture, though, provides a throughline between her own artistic past, Native histories and beliefs, and Confluence's goal of connecting people to the Indigenous peoples of the Columbia Plateau.

Structural Colonialism

Indian displacement, depopulation and relocation, and settler colonial commercial development in what would become the Western United States were complementary dynamics. Patrick Wolfe describes settler colonialism as a "structure," as opposed to an event. It has "both negative and positive dimensions," by which he means it strives to eradicate and erase (negative) while simultaneously laying a foundation for, and ultimately justifying, the developmental conditions for the new colonial society to flourish (positive, or perhaps it is more appropriate to say "generative"). (Wolfe 1999, 393) Rather than viewing colonization as a series of historical markers, Wolfe and others see it as an unfolding process, a slow normalization of codes and conventions reliant on apparatuses of the state, especially legal and juridical, that also deploys cultural and representational strategies to fulfill its ends. Elimination and removal are contingent upon dehumanization in the form of linguistic and visual signifiers that render colonized peoples as ignorant, savage, and backward. The pernicious effects of a belief that Native Americans exist outside of history were (and are) carefully constructed and maintained to support systems of dominance. They are products of deliberate and willful choices and decisions made by real people. Once such systems are in place, however, they become normalized and rendered invisible.

Indigenous arts scholar Dylan Robinson builds upon Wolfe's theory by arguing that settler colonialism creates "particular assemblages of unmarked structures of certainty that guide normative perception and may enact epistemic violence." (Robinson 2020, 9) In other words, new affective modes of experiencing space and place create and internalize the colonizing subject, even within the experience of the colonized. Robinson's analysis is about sound, a topic I will discuss in the next chapter, but his statement clearly encompasses the many sensorial dimensions through which we understand the world. The sights, sounds, smells, and feel of Fort Vancouver and its surroundings have changed irrevocably over the last two centuries. But how often do people actually consider such changes? Confluence's Land Bridge acknowledges this transformation and provides a guide for reperceiving the location. Its design deliberately unsettles these strategies by visibly foregrounding the many tribal languages as part of the sculptural environment, reintroducing riparian plant species in and around the bridge, and creating a pathway with overlooks that ask viewers to connect the past and present of this particular place.

In *Decolonizing Methodologies: Research and Indigenous Peoples*, Tuhiwai Smith demonstrates how colonialism and Western modes of knowledge production are ideological projects that collude in the erasure of voices, histories, and ways of understanding.

> For the indigenous world, Western conceptions of space, of arrangements and display, of the relationship between people and the landscape, of culture as an object of study, have meant that not only has the indigenous world been represented in particular ways back to the West, but the indigenous world view, the land and the people, have been radically transformed in the spatial image of the West...Land, for example, was viewed as something to be tamed and brought under control. The landscape, the arrangement of nature, could be altered by 'Man': swamps could be drained, waterways diverted, inshore areas filled, not simply for physical survival, but for further exploitation of the environment or making it 'more pleasing' aesthetically.
>
> (Smith 2012, 53)

Tuhiwai Smith enumerates an attitude toward land that still determines our interactions with nature and the environment. Nature is there to be tamed, dominated, and brought under control so that humans can exist within it more efficiently and so that its resources can be exploited to make our lives better. Two centuries of "progress" have brought us to a point of no return, however. The climate crisis is upon us because we have forgotten how to live in a sustainable relationship with nature and the environment.

Note

1 KPFF, a major design and engineering firm, was brought on as a consultant. Rene Senos, ASLA, was project manager and landscape architect for Jones & Jones. Claire Enlow, "Prairie Crossing," Landscape Architecture, Feb. 2009, pp. 2–7.

References

Boyd, Robert T. 1999. *Indians, Fire, and the Land in the Pacific Northwest*. Corvallis, OR: Oregon State University Press.

Enlow, Clair. 2009. "Prairie Crossing." *Landscape Architecture*.

"Confluence Podcast: Vancouver Story Gathering." 2020 *Confluence Project* (blog). Accessed September 30, 2023. https://www.confluenceproject.org/library-post/confluence-podcast-vancouver-story-gathering/.

"Confluence Project Records", WCMss444, Whitman College and Northwest Archives. https://archiveswest.orbiscascade.org/ark:/80444/xv285430

Daehnke, Jon. 2018. "Reflections on the Confluence Project." In *A Museum Studies Approach to Heritage*, edited by Sheila Watson, Amy Jane Barnes, and Katy Bunning, 1st ed., 559–69. Abingdon, Oxon ; New York, NY : Routledge, 2018. | Series: Leicester readers in museum studies: Routledge. https://doi.org/10.4324/9781315668505-43.

Deur, Douglas. 2012. "An Ethnohistorical Overview of Groups with Ties to Fort Vancouver National Historic Site." Accessed June 28, 2023. https://works.bepress.com/douglas_deur/45/.

Fisheries, NOAA. 2022. "Rebuilding Interior Columbia Basin Salmon and Steelhead | NOAA Fisheries." NOAA. West Coast. Accessed September 30, 2022. https://www.fisheries.noaa.gov/resource/document/rebuilding-interior-columbia-basin-salmon-and-steelhead.

Hunn, Eugene S. 1990. *Nch'i-Wána, 'the Big River': Mid-Columbia Indians and Their Land*. Seattle, WA: University of Washington Press.

Hunt, H. F. 1918. "Slavery among the Indians of Northwest America." *The Washington Historical Quarterly* 9 (4): 277–83.

Lansing, Jewel Beck. 2003. *Portland: People, Politics, and Power, 1851–2001*. Corvallis, OR: Oregon State University Press.

Lewis, Meriwether, Clark, William, et al. March 30, 1806 entry in The Journals of the Lewis and Clark Expedition, ed. Gary Moulton. Lincoln, NE: University of Nebraska Press / University of Nebraska-Lincoln Libraries-Electronic Text Center, 2005. http://lewisandclarkjournals.unl.edu/journals.php?id=1806-09-04.

Maben, Manly. 1987. *Vanport*. Portland, OR: Oregon Historical Society Press.

McClure, Richard. 1978. *An Archaeological Survey of Petroglyph and Pictograph Sites in the State of Washington*. Archaeological Reports of Investigation, No.1. Entry #: 45 KL 58. The Evergreen State College.

National Park Service. 2002. "Fort Vancouver National Historic Site Draft General Management Plan Environmental Impact Statement." Box 10, Folder 12. WCMss. 444.

Northwest Power and Conservation Council, "Aluminum." n.d. Accessed September 30, 2023. https://www.nwcouncil.org/reports/columbia-river-history/aluminum/.

"November 6, 1805 | Journals of the Lewis and Clark Expedition." n.d. Accessed September 27, 2023. https://lewisandclarkjournals.unl.edu/item/lc.jrn.1805-11-06#lc.jrn.1805-11-06.04.

Parks, Shoshi. 2018, March 18. "York Explored the West with Lewis and Clark, But His Freedom Wouldn't Come Until Decades Later." *Smithsonian Magazine*. Accessed September 30, 2023.

Ramsey, Jarold. 1977. *Coyote Was Going There: Indian Literature of the Oregon Country*. Seattle, WA: University of Washington Press.

Robinson, Dylan. 2020. "Hungry Listening: Resonant Theory for Indigenous Sound Studies." *Indigenous Americas*. Minneapolis, MN: University of Minnesota Press.

Ross, Alexander. 1904. *Ross's Adventures of the First Settlers on the Oregon or Columbia River, 1810–1813*. Vol. 7. A. H. Clark.

Smith, Linda Tuhiwai. 2012. *Decolonizing Methodologies: Research and Indigenous Peoples*. London: Zed Books.

Taylor, Sue. 2000. Lillian Pitt at the Museum at Warm Springs. *Art in America* 88(3): 139.

"Vancouver Land Bridge Art." n.d. *Confluence Project* (blog). Accessed September 30, 2023. https://www.confluenceproject.org/library-post/vancouver-land-bridge-art/.

Wolfe, Patrick. 1999. "Settler Colonialism and the Transformation of Anthropology: The Politics and Poetics of an Ethnographic Event." *Writing Past Colonialism Series*. London: Cassell.

3   The Bird Blind at Sandy River Delta

A Confluence of Sounds

"We have a confluence of sounds." So said Jane Jacobsen on the morning of the dedication of the Land Bridge at Fort Vancouver. An article in the Vancouver Columbian described the Confluence CEO's attempts to be heard over the noises of trains, the highway, and fighter jets from nearby Portland International Airport. ("Land Bridge, Five Years Old, Draws People to Crossroads, Meeting Place" 2013) Later that day, Jacobsen, Maya Lin, and other supporters of the Confluence Project would make the half-hour drive east to Sandy River Delta, a part of the Columbia River Gorge National Scenic Area, to dedicate the Bird Blind, the third completed installation. If Chapters 1 and 2 ended by exploring how Lin's work can help us reperceive the environmental effects of climate change, this chapter will focus on a specific, overlooked aspect of the Confluence Project that performs this function: sound. Sound is a dominant motif of the installations and earthworks at all of the Confluence sites. Sacajawea State Park is characterized by seven basalt listening circles. Cape Disappointment and Chief Timothy Park feature amphitheaters. Sandy River Delta's Bird Blind symbolizes provides a shelter for quiet encounters between birds, humans, and other animal species. Earlier proposals for the unfinished installation at Celilo Park called for a small pavilion that plays a looped recording of the roaring falls made before they were inundated by the construction of The Dalles Dam in 1957. Sound's prominence within the Confluence Project is a reoccurring theme throughout Lin's oeuvre, found in pieces like *The Listening Cone* (2009), a permanent sculptural installation at the California Academy of Sciences in San Francisco, and *What is Missing* (2009–), an ongoing, multimedia project that confronts viewers with the imagery and sounds of endangered species recorded in their natural habitats.

Transformation of the landscape is also an intervention in the soundscape. R. Murray Schafer who coined the word "soundscape" equates this intervention with empire, an association that often goes overlooked in histories of the term. "In the West the ear has given way to the eye as the most

DOI: 10.4324/9781003309024-4

important gatherer of environmental information ... The huge noises of our civilization are the result of imperialistic ambitions." (Cox and Warner 2004, 36) Elsewhere, Edward Said advocates for interpreting this soundscape through a postcolonial framework, or "contrapuntally." The voices, music, and rituals of colonized peoples have all-too-often been silenced by imperial expansion. Said asks us to reread the "cultural archive ... not univocally but contrapuntally, with a simultaneous awareness both of the metropolitan history that is narrated and of those other histories against which (and together with which) the dominating discourse acts." (Said 1993, 50–51) The Confluence Project has created spaces where many of the sounds of Indigenous peoples and species have occurred, been performed, recorded, or made available to a broader public. Listening to these soundscapes yields a contrapuntal interpretation of shared ecological transformations. The sounds of rural industrialization produced along the Columbia River by railroad tracks and drawbridges, highways, cars, trucks, tourists, and park visitors must be heard contrapuntally as human phenomena that simultaneously produce the eerie silences of toxic plumes, pollution, and the slow quieting of species extinction. This chapter will argue that by calling attention to the soundscapes of the Columbia region, the Confluence Project sites encourage visitors to *hear and see* the courses of empire upon which the Anthropocene was built.

The Bird Blind

The Sandy River is fed by glacial melt and lahar runoff from nearby Mt. Hood. It travels west toward Portland for half of its approximately 250-mile distance before it veers north until it meets the Columbia. Sandy River Delta was home or familiar to numerous Native American bands.[1] In between 1806 and 1855, increasingly large numbers of White settlers from the eastern United States began to emigrate following the discovery in 1812 of a wagon-safe route over the Continental Divide and along the Columbia River which became the Oregon Trail. In addition to fur traders and fortune seekers, waves of missionaries made the journey west to establish missions and devotional enclaves in the hopes of converting Native populations to Christianity. Lewis and Clark estimated the "Clackamas" (the identifier that appears frequently in the journals) numbered 1800 members in 1806 but by the time of the Treaty of 1855 which dispossessed tribal nations in the Pacific Northwest of tens of millions of acres of land and relocated Plateau peoples to small, remote reservations, it is thought that only 88 Indians survived. (Deloria 2012) The interim period witnessed the Great Migration of 1843 following passage of a bill to grant over 600 acres to "every White male." Migration created increasingly hostile altercations between settlers and Native Americans, culminating in the Whitman Massacre of 1847. Members of the Cayuse tribe attacked and killed Marcus and Narcissa Whitman, along with 11 of their followers at the Whitman Mission near Fort Walla Walla. The massacre was predicated by a measles outbreak brought by the White settlers that killed up to half of the local Cayuse tribe. Following Whitman's death, local militias carried out a series of raids against tribal members that culminated in the hanging of five members chosen to "stand in" for the Cayuse who carried out the initial killings. The Whitman cause was quickly utilized by White landowners and the federal government to advance land-grab policies and further eradicate Indians. (Kaeding 2010)

Like nearby Vancouver, Sandy River Delta's geological character made it highly suitable for heavy industry. The industrialization of the region that took place over the course of a century led to the near collapse and extinction of numerous animal species. River barges hauled lumber and wheat through the region. Factorized canning turned fisheries into big businesses. Railroads made connecting the agricultural and logging regions in and around the Gorge even faster beginning in the mid-nineteenth century. Clear-cutting made way for use of the land for farming. More farming and the growth of Portland as a vital regional shipping hub fed the thirst for water. The first hydroelectric dam in the Northwest was built in Spokane in 1885. Over the next century, the Columbia and Snake Rivers would see the construction of dozens of projects rerouting the major tributaries for commercial transportation, agriculture, and hydropower. Megaliths like Bonneville, Grand Coulee, The Dalles, and John Day forever altered the topography of the region with a corresponding devastation of species. In 1941, the Aluminum Company of America (ALCOA) built an aluminum reduction plant that supplied the US military with lightweight metal used to make airplanes during World War II. Following the War, the plant was purchased by the Reynolds company and grew to become one of the major employers in the region. But this growth came at a cost: by the late 1960s, the plant was a target of environmental lawsuits and eventually declared a Superfund site by the Environmental Protection Agency. In 1991, Reynolds sold the plant "for public use" and the Port of Portland invested $14 million in environmental reclamation projects. It is currently managed by the US Forest Service. (Nesbit 2007)

Lin and the Confluence Project team were attracted to this site, in part, because of an ongoing, regional riparian reforestation program overseen by the U.S. Department of Agriculture and National Forest Service. The NFS was also focused on restoration of the riverine ecosystem that included the removal of two dams, the Marmot Dam and the smaller Little Sandy River Diversion Dam, both built around 1912 by Portland Gas and Electric to supply hydropower to the nearby city. (Jacobsen and Harkenridder, n.d.) Their removal in 2007–2008 was one of several, more ambitious efforts to restore the entire watershed basin. ("Sandy River" n.d.) A happy coincidence of timing resulted in both dams coming offline just as the Fort Vancouver and Sandy River Confluence sites were dedicated. A smaller dike between the Columbia and Sandy channels was removed a few years later in 2013. To date, the Sandy River's recovery basin has been an ecological success story, with increased salmon and trout populations and self-sustaining habitat restoration, including a revival of wapato, a wetland tuber that was a crucial staple of regional Native American diets. (Archuleta and Norton 2021)

The 1500-acre park sits on a floodplain managed by the U.S. Forest Service close to the city of Troutdale, an ex-urb of Portland. The site has long been a popular recreational destination with a complex trail system used for hunting, fishing, horseback riding, and dog walking. Planning for the Bird Blind began in 2006 and by then, it was no longer feasible to complete all the installations within the 2004–2006 Bicentennial timeframe. It is difficult to pinpoint an exact moment when a decision to delay was finalized or whether the slow process of creating public art just had to be accepted. Early documentation in the archives indicates that completion of seven extant sites by 2006 was the goal from the outset. (Box 3, Folder 55, "Confluence Project Records", WCMss444, Whitman College and Northwest Archives) But locations that were initially favored, like an installation at Frenchman's Bar, began to drop out of contention. Additionally, conceptual and fundraising delays, staffing turnover, and the sheer bureaucratic scale of collaborating with dozens of state and federal agencies, grants foundations, non-profits, and tribal nations and advisers made the initial deadline impossible. By the time that design plans, budgets, and approvals were set, the goal for completion was October 2007, a date that had to be pushed even further. In conjunction with the Bird Blind, the park would also get an upgrade to its supporting infrastructure, including a new dedicated offramp on Interstate 84, improved landscaping and trail maintenance, and removal of some invasive plant species.

Looking at (and around) the Bird Blind

A 1.2-mile gravel trail leads from the parking lot past groves of Black Cottonwood trees interspersed with Oregon ash and Bigleaf maple, alongside giant electrical transmission towers, clusters of Himalayan Blackberry bushes, open meadows with prairie grasses, picnic tables, and a wide variety of other native and non-native plants. Unobtrusive trail signage directs visitors to the Confluence path that intersects with two additional meandering, unpaved paths. All roads lead to the Bird Blind; however, the multiple routes encourage exploration of the park and its access to the rivers and channels. Shortly after its dedication and before the trail markers were improved, it was easy to get lost. During previous trips, I found myself watching and hearing dogs play fetch at the water's edge, planes landing and taking off from nearby Troutdale airport, stumbling on a small forest's worth of discarded Christmas trees, and the sounds of the interstate mingling with flowing water, the occasional wood-pecker, birdsong, and the rustle of critters through the surrounding brush. I take the time to highlight this intermixing of sounds and sights to emphasize again the multi-sensorial experience of the contemporary industrialized land- and soundscapes.

A wooden entrance ramp curves slowly through a grove of Oregon ash planted at opposite sides so that the structure can't be seen directly from the trail. Lin was very specific about wanting visitors to encounter the Blind gradually. Landscaping and location were used to discourage direct access or a command-ing viewpoint of the enclosure. Instead, the Blind should be "slowly revealed to [visitors] as they approached the end of the ramp." (Box 9, Folder 13, "Conflu-ence Project Records", WCMss444, Whitman College and Northwest Archives) A single line of text carved into the handrail explains why this specific location was chosen and its importance as a campsite for the Corps of Discovery carved into the ramp's handrail. At the end of the ramp, visitors take a sharp right turn and cross a five-foot bridge to enter the Bird Blind. This highly choreographed encounter creates a sense of mystery and surprise, perhaps mimicking or em-bodying experiences of the explorers and their crew. It also acclimatizes viewers to the quiet and solitude necessary for the Bird Blind to function as it was meant.

Frequently described as an "elliptical structure," the Bird Blind is approxi-mately 150 square feet in size and sits atop a concrete and steel foundation of four piers Figure 3.1. It is perched (the avian metaphors write themselves) on a

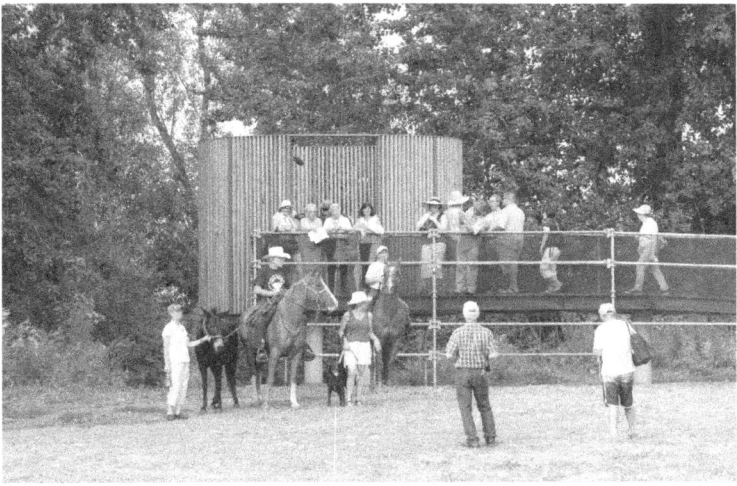

Figure 3.1 The Bird Blind at Sandy River Delta during Dedication Ceremony, 2008.

Sources: Confluence 2018-021-31. WCMss444. Confluence Project Records. Whitman College and Northwest Archives.

terraced embankment overlooking a short channel that connects the Columbia River with the Sandy River to the west. Lin's original plan called for the structure to be built on the steep river bank, a design ultimately discouraged by park officials, who argued that the structure would be better protected from frequent flooding and future bank erosion. Removing the dams and dike to restore the channel meant that the Blind would have to be built a few feet from the edge to account for these factors. Lin was initially resistant but allowed for compromise once she was assured by park officials that relocating the Blind would "not work against the dynamic riverine system, and will be more in harmony with the natural system." (Box 9, Folder 15, "Confluence Project Records", WCMss444, Whitman College and Northwest Archives) The solution was to design an elegant cantilevered support that would allow the foundation to be anchored to the more stable flat terrace while extending out toward the slope of the riverbank.

While the exterior is both striking and unassuming, it is the interior of the structure that performs much of the labor of this artwork. The entrance is a doorless steel frame the same width as the bridgeway, accommodating two bodies but encouraging one-at-a-time. The structure has no roof—it is open to the elements. Inside, the "walls" are 105 uniform wooden beams carved from black locust trees and arranged at 3-inch intervals equidistantly around the circumference, save for the entrance. Each beam is carved with the name of an animal or bird species recorded during the two-year journey, with the first entry from May 18, 1804 ("Horned Lizard") and the last on August 7, 1806 ("White Gull"). The slats are installed chronologically from left-to-right so that the list can be read "in order" by making a sharp left turn upon entering the blind. The text is oriented vertically and records the date of observation, the common name, scientific name, and current status of each entry (species of concern, endangered, extinct, or blank for unchanged). For example, on April 7, 1806, as the Corps was camped near the current Sandy River location, Lewis wrote a lengthy entry describing how "Reubin Field," an expedition member, "killed a bird of the Quail kind that was whistling near our camp." (Lewis, et al., April 7, 1806 entry in The Journals of the Lewis and Clark Expedition 2005) Above "Quail" is written the common name, "Mountain Quail," followed by "Oreortyx pictus," the scientific identification, and, finally, the status of the species at the time of the Blind's completion; in this case, it is a "Species of Concern." If an animal remains present in its habitat, the space next to the scientific name is left blank. At the time of the site's dedication, over a third of the species listed had become extinct, or were listed as endangered or a species of concern.

The experience of the enclosure from the inside promotes a feeling of loss and melancholy, two affects with which Lin's memorial work is often associated. The Bird Blind's use of text, the archival listing of species, and the curated choreography it compels from the viewer all bear a striking resemblance to the Vietnam Veteran's Memorial, Lin's most iconic work Figure 3.2. Marita Sturken writes that with the Vietnam Veteran's Memorial, "the names form a loop, beginning as they do at the central hinge of the memorial and moving

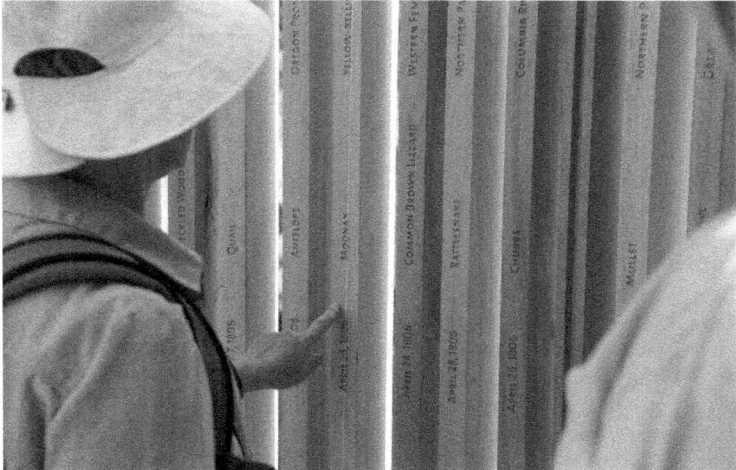

Figure 3.2 Interior of the Bird Blind featuring species encountered and recorded in the journals of Lewis and Clark, date of journal entry, common name, and current status.

Sources: Confluence 2018-021-31. WCMss444. Confluence Project Records. Whitman College and Northwest Archives.

out on the right wall, then continuing at the far end of the left wall and moving toward the center." (Sturken 1991, 128) In other words, the names of the first soldiers to die are stacked at the center of the work alongside those of the last recorded deaths. There are 58,318 names etched on the work's polished black granite surfaces. For Sturken, this arrangement represents the scale of loss and the rippling historical currents that move beyond the timeframe of the Vietnam War. There is no right or wrong way to read the list of names for visitors to the Memorial and each name evokes not just one individual but the many lives, eras, and events touched by their deaths. Lin describes the viewer experience of the Memorial as a "journey." Those who read the wall chronologically travel in a loop that encourages a panoramic view of the Mall and its surroundings. Others might descend to the middle axis and then ascend to the opposite end, taking in the monuments of the Mall, the Capitol building, and the other nearby memorials, reinforcing the fact that the pain and anguish of the deceased veterans, their friends and families were the product of decisions made by other human beings in the nearby buildings. Such a journey thus makes the Memorial part of a much larger system, a holistic ecology of state power. The apparatus of the American government is implicated in the deaths of its citizens, and the reflective granite surfaces absorb viewers into the work itself, another reminder of the War's lingering presence.

This journey echoes a similar choreographed pattern at all of the Confluence sites, including the Bird Blind. The curving ramp and circular orientation require viewers to take in a 360-degree view of the surroundings. Species are listed chronologically, as opposed to alphabetically. Visitors entering the structure face the "middle" of the list, or those species recorded around 1805 by Lewis and Clark, discouraging an immediate linear experience of time and history. As park officials noted, the connection between "past and present observations of the world around us forms the fundamental vision for the art work." (Jacobsen and Harkenridder n.d., Box 9, Folder 15) This temporal disjuncture is complimented by a spatial one, as well. The Bird Blind is, ultimately, a platform to see and hear the Delta's biodiversity and its supporting ecosystem. The porous arrangement of the slats disrupts the otherwise fixed boundaries between inside and outside. Here, too, the text reinforces this relationship by asking visitors to read upward, toward the sky and the surrounding tree canopy. Like the Vietnam Veteran's Memorial, the text is carved into the surface of each slat, creating a negative space. Absence is felt at a material level, reminding us of the precarious status of many of the species or their complete disappearance as a result of the River's development as an extractive resource.

There is one final element of the Bird Blind to which I want to call attention. In one of the early sketches Lin made at the site, she identifies "sustainable cedar" as the material to be used for the slats. ("Confluence Project Records—Archives West" 2018, Box 9, Folder 9) Cedar trees are common to Oregon and Washington and can be found in and around the Columbia River Gorge and Sandy River Delta. White cedar was found in abundance and noted in the logs of both Captain Clark and Sergeant Gass. In addition to the trees already mentioned in this chapter, a plant survey conducted by Confluence partners Greg Archuleta and Jesse Norton identified dozens of other species and provided recommendations about which would be more resilient to the impacts of global warming. Cedars are also thirsty trees, requiring lots of water, and are thus susceptible to drought and wildfire of the kind that have become more common over the past decade. For reasons that are unclear from the archival record, black locust was chosen for the slats. It may be that locust is more durable or easier to work with from a woodworking standpoint. However, locust is also an invasive species, non-native to the region and the Pacific Northwest. The artist acknowledges this fact in a short entry about the Sandy River Delta in her book *Maya Lin: Topologies*. (Lin 2015, 372) Whether or not this was an intentional, aesthetic decision, a practical one, or some combination of the two, is unknown. The poignancy of deploying an invasive hardwood tree as the primary material for composition of the Bird Blind, a work about colonial surveyors and soldiers traveling in a foreign (to them) land in preparation for trade, and later conquest, is itself a powerful metaphor for the Confluence Project's own goal of commemorating the afterlife of the Corps of Discovery's expedition and the two centuries of environmental and ecological transformation that followed in its wake.

Listening to the Sandy River Delta

Lewis and Clark recorded their arrival at what they called "Quick Sand" river on November 3, 1805, on their way to the Pacific. They thought they had found a major waterway but were informed by Indians that it was runoff from nearby Mt. Hood. Geologists have since determined that a major eruption had occurred 20 years earlier and that the murky, slow waters and volumes of sediment disgorged by the eruption helped form the "Island" of the Sandy River Delta. These conditions also made the area a thriving avian habitat. Birds appear everywhere in the journal entries of all the Corps members, both as a source of food and fascination. They saw "Swan, geese, Brants, Cranes, Stalks [*NB: Storks*], white guls, comerants & plevers &c." (Lewis, et al., April 7, 1806 entry in The Journals of the Lewis and Clark Expedition 2005) On the journey back east, they "Saw the Log cock, the hummingbird, gees ducks &c today...we saw the martin, small gees, the small speckled woodpecker with a white back, the Blue crested Corvus, ravens, crows, eagles Vultures and hawks." And it was here that Private Field, the expedition's best marksman, killed the whistling quail, prompting an uncharacteristically rapturous description from Clark. He calls it "a most butifull bird" after a detailed accounting of its defining features, the two long feathers that extend over 2 inches from the top of the head, and its resemblance to a partridge, except for its plumage, which "differs in every part." The underbody contained a "bright dove colored blue" and the neck a "fine dark brick red." "... a wide Stripe which extends from Side to Side of the body and occupies the lower region of the breast is beautifully varigated with the brick red white & black which predominates ... and the Colours mark the feathers transversely." Twelve dark brown feathers of equal length make up the tail. Near the end of the entry, Lewis describes the birdcall. He states that "it's loud note it Single and Consists of a loud Squall, intirely different from the whistling of our partridge or quailes. it has a chiping note when allarmed like our partridge.—", before going on to say that a second bird of this kind was killed later that day. (Lewis, et al., April 6, 1806 entry in The Journals of the Lewis and Clark Expedition 2005)

This finely observed description of the Mountain Quail mentioned above contrasts sharply with Clark's complaints about the "emensely numerous" number of waterfowl whose "horrid" noise kept him awake while camped at Sandy River. Confluence frequently uses this reference in its description of the Bird Blind as a way to contextualize the site. This avian habitat remains part of a much larger, robust ecosystem of the Lower Columbia River. It is a crucial rest stop for migratory birds along the Pacific Flyway between Alaska and South America. The expedition spent a week at this location hunting and drying meat to store until they reached the Nez Perce lands. Journal entries describe starving Indian families migrating west. A late winter had disrupted traditional salmon runs. Corps members killed elk, deer, and a bear, in addition to geese and ducks. The crew was also fond of dog meat. On August 13,

Lewis wrote: "the dog now constitutes a considerable part of our subsistence and with most of the party has become a favorite food; certain I am that it is a healthy strong diet, and from habit it has become by no means disagreeable to me, I prefer it to lean venison or Elk, and is very far superior to the horse in any state." (Lewis, et al., April 13, 1806 entry in The Journals of the Lewis and Clark Expedition 2005) This excerpt is understandably not publicized at a location that is well-known as a dog park. As the passages written at Sandy River Delta indicate, birds were a vital source of food for Corps members. But their abundance could also be a source of aggravation. Clark's annoyance at the constant squawking might elicit sympathy from contemporary readers. It certainly expresses a modern understanding of birds, which takes their presence and noise for granted.

The alarming decline in global avian populations due to numerous factors, in particular a loss of habitat, echoes Clark's conflicted relationship with birds. Birds are major sources of the global diet, especially poultry and eggs. In urban spaces, the animals can be nuisances requiring modification of buildings or statues to prevent nesting or unsightly defecation. In rural areas, avian migration and feeding patterns can damage crop fields or devastate seed plantings. But birds are also endless sources of fascination. Duck and quail hunting, for food and sport, remain popular in the United States. Likewise, bird watching is currently a booming leisure activity, albeit one primarily associated with a wealthier, Whiter demographic. Birds are pets and companions, curiosities, and objects of study and fascination in zoos and aviaries. Lin's Bird Blind connotes the many contradictions upon which humans construct their relationship with these animals. The structure is educational and asks viewers to register the loss of species and habitats through quiet watching and listening. As a didactic structure, Lin's Blind can never be entirely divorced from extractive empiricism and scientific rationalism that understand birds as objects of and for human study, consumption, and pleasure. The fact that bird blinds are frequently used for this purpose and also for hunting and killing is part of their functional layers of meaning. The specter of death is always present in some form within a bird blind.

Frightening statistics about dramatic declines in avian populations around the globe are starting to disrupt our capacity to take these creatures for granted; 2023 has seen an outbreak of a more deadly avian flu virus, one that threatens to become endemic or even jump species. The pathogenic H5N1 virus devastated chicken populations in industrialized meat processing plants but was found to be pervasive in the wild and was recently categorized as a cross-species transmission when discovered as the cause of death in some marine mammals. ("Study of H5N1 Avian Flu Seal Deaths Reveals Multiple Lineages | CIDRAP" 2023) The Guardian reported in late 2022 that "49% of bird species are declining, one in eight are threatened with extinction and at least 187 species are confirmed or suspected to have gone extinct since 1500." (Weston 2022) An article that appeared in the peer-reviewed scientific journal

Global Change Biology focused specifically on the Pacific Northwest region, noting that bird species decline patterns are synergistically produced; in other words, there are multiple factors. Habitat loss is the immediate cause of bird deaths, but habitat cannot be uncoupled from a loss of mature forest, disappearance of intact ecological, self-sustaining landscapes, warming, reduced precipitation, loss of seral (or intermediate stage) broadleaf forest that facilitates breeding and foraging, etc.

What the authors call "synergistic" might, in the humanities and social sciences, be labeled "interdisciplinary," in that one symptom of decline cannot be separated from its many multiple causes. The collapse of bird species is, to use another term, overdetermined. The trail to the Bird Blind at Sandy River Delta, as previously described, takes visitors past open fields, trees and plants, rivers, and streams. There is also no section of this landscape unimpacted by human activity. Those same transmission towers alluded to earlier along the trail to the Bird Blind account for an unknown number of bird deaths. Browsing for books about birdsong in my campus library, I happened on a collection of papers published in 1978 by the U.S. Department of Interior, Fish and Wildlife Service. "Transmission lines seem to have two kinds of effects on birds: physical and electromagnetic." [Willard 1978, 5] The event concluded by acknowledging that such towers did create disruptions for bird populations and were a significant cause of death. But it stated that more studies were needed. This workshop was held at a moment when the Environmental Protection Agency and Clean Water Act were only a few years old. Now we have more data, a more complete picture of what is happening, and yet solutions and actions seem as distant and quiet as they did nearly 50 years ago.

Soundscapes to Sound Art

"Aarrrrt ... ARRTTTT ... Ah-ah-ARTschwager!!" So begins conceptual artist and photographer Louise Lawler's 1972 performance "Birdcalls." What sounds like a screeching crow or raven bellows the barely discernible last name of Richard Artschwager, a sculptor who rose to fame alongside Pop and Minimalist artists the decade prior to Lawler's invocation. For the next six-and-a-half minutes, Lawler vocalizes the names of 28 well-known contemporaneous artists as if they were spoken or sung by a host of imaginary bird-like creatures. Not intended to mimic actual bird species (or maybe I should say that none of the calls are specifically recognizable to someone with no ornithological training like me), each name does sound bird-like in its individuation. Vito Acconci is rendered in staccato bursts, a high chirping "Vito," followed by a slightly more drawn-out "Con-CHI" rising at the end to reflect the Italian pronunciation of his surname. Julian Schnabel is pronounced as if from the low grumbling growl of a sick rooster: "Schnaaaabull." The tone of the recording has an eerie, echoey quality, part playful homage, part cutting critique, perhaps owing to the fact that the list is a who's-who of canonical post-war artists, exclusively male. Lawler devised this sound art piece with her colleague and friend, Martha Kite, as a way to ward off would-be attackers when they were walking home from the Westside Manhattan piers late at night. (Allan 2009, 109) I first heard the work while walking through the gardens at Dia:Beacon. It played at a low volume over the loudspeakers and was difficult to distinguish from actual bird sounds unless and until you knew what you were listening to or noticed the looping repetition. Lawler's brilliant, laugh-out-loud, inside joke was also a sly feminist critique of the male-dominated artworld of her era. I have no wish to elide the importance of that critique. Such an analysis is beyond the scope of this book. Instead, I want to briefly focus on the emergence of sound art as a cross-disciplinary practice (one nevertheless indebted to feminist artistic strategies) in the 1960s and beyond, and its importance for the place-based, site-specific art of Lin's Confluence Project.

Thom Holmes defines sound art as "any artwork that makes use of the idea of sound, the experience or perception of sound, the physical effect of sound, or the residual traces of sonic activity as its primary material." (Holmes 2022, 1) This would seem to imply a very broad category of work that might even include traditional fine arts practices (painting, sculpture, architecture) if the conditions in which it is encountered (gallery installation, outdoor setting, etc.) are also taken into account. But the author adds a caveat: a work should also be considered sound art if it does any of the above and "does not fit squarely within the confines and traditions of existing artistic genres." This qualification, as Holmes notes, can often make the task of identifying and labeling something "sound art" challenging. The same can be said of the Confluence Project. Sound is never overtly foregrounded at any of the extant sites. Sonic materiality is instead sublimated at these sites. Lin beckons us to hear the broader context and surroundings of each location, but sound is a *secondary* material. It is used to reinforce the artist's larger goal of reorienting the senses as a way of perceiving the environment differently.

Sound was crucial to early twentieth-century European avant-garde practitioners in the Futurist and Dada movements. F.T. Marinetti's Zang Tumb Tumb (1914) used inventive typography and onomatopoeia to recreate the sounds of mechanization and industrialization on the printed page and in performance. Luigi Russolo's manifesto The Art of Noise (1913) was published a year earlier and expanded musical vocabularies to incorporate the sonic landscapes of a rapidly urbanizing society. Hugo Ball's poetic recitations of invented, non-sensical terms and phrases in works like Karawane (1915) echoed Marinetti's experiments with wordplay but were performed live in front of audiences at Zurich's Cabaret Voltaire. Both Ball and his partner/collaborator Emmy Hemmings, herself a poet, were foundational Dada figures. Where Futurism embraced the modernization and technological advancements of the period, Dada rejected the blind conformity to Western teleological logic, reason, and progress that led to the horrors of World War I. In their own way, both of these iconic movements were early incarnations of an environmental sound art practice *avant la lettre*.

The work of John Cage is closer to Lin's practice in its embrace of Eastern philosophies and ecological concerns. David Ingram explains how Cage's interest in Zen Buddhism and a growing awareness of ecological damage informed the artist's philosophies on music and the environment. In the 1960s, Cage's positions became more radical as he embraced what Ingram labels "eco-anarchism." "We've poisoned our food, polluted our air and water, killed birds and cattle, eliminated forests, impoverished, eroded the earth," he was quoted as saying in the interview collection For the Birds (1976). (Ingram 2023) Cage promoted environmental awareness following the publication of Rachel Carson's Silent Spring in 1962. Carson's text was instrumental in galvanizing grassroots activism that helped transform public policy, most notably through the establishment of the Environmental Protection Agency a decade later. Silent Spring's title is itself an allusion to sound, or rather, the absence of birdsong due to the proliferation of toxic chemicals used in large-scale agricultural production. The book begins: "It was a spring without voices. On the mornings that had once throbbed with the dawn chorus of robins, catbirds, doves, jays, wrens, and scores of other bird voices there was now no sound; only silence lay over the fields and woods and marsh." (Gilmurray 2016, 74) His later writings on the environment and ecology (which he considered part of his artistic practice) would inspire compositions like Bird Cage (1972) that utilized tape recordings of birdsong from a Pennsylvania aviary and a Delaware wildlife refuge. These works represented an advanced formulation of music and ecology as entities indistinguishable from one another: "nature is not a separation of water from air, or of the sky from the earth, etc., but a 'working-together,' or a 'playing-together' of those elements. That is what we call ecology. Music, as I conceive it, is ecological. You could go further and say that it IS ecology." (Ingram 2023)

Artist and historian Brandon LaBelle analyzes Cage's influence on movements and groups that began to experiment with sound in the 1960s and 1970s. Allan Kaprow's Happenings generally incorporated the social sounds of the artmaking and viewing as part of the work itself. Fluxus, a loose collective of international artists with affiliations to Dada, worked in performance, a hybrid of composition and choreography labeled "scores," which were generally a series of short instructions that frequently involved speech, music, and noise. While sound did not feature as much in Minimalist sculpture, a work like Robert Morris's Box with the Sound of Its Own Making (1961) stands out. Recorded noises of saws and hammers play via a cassette tape hidden in a small, polished walnut box, an auditorial exposure of the means of its own production, even as it is visually concealed. Hans Haacke's Condensation Cubes (1963–1965) were Plexiglas boxes containing water and attuned to the gallery's environment. At certain temperatures and intervals depending on the temperature of the surroundings, they would produce condensation and evaporation. This liquid, according to James Nisbet, would "steam, drip, sway, and plop." (Nisbet 2014, 202) Nisbet quotes Haacke:

> A 'sculpture' that physically reacts to its environment and/or affects its surroundings is no longer to be regarded as an object. The range of outside factors influencing it, as well as its own radius of action, reach beyond the space it materially occupies. It thus merges with the environment in a relationship that is better understood as a 'system' of interdependent processes.
>
> (Nisbet 2014, 202–3)

Works like Morris's Box and Haacke's Cubes are emblematic of Minimalism and Conceptualism. As such, they advance the era's concerns with how artwork functions as part of a larger interdependent system of museums, galleries, curators, staff, publicity, criticism and scholarship, viewers and patrons, etc. Institutional critique emerges as a reaction to these systems. Performance art and video's adoption by women artists is used to carve out space within an otherwise male-dominated artworld. Sound plays a vital, if still undertheorized role in advancing the era's creative practices. Artists embraced these new tools and processes to dislocate themselves from galleries and museums (to an extent) and utilize the natural world as site, setting, and material. The results were extravagant, profound, and unsettling, from the monumental sculptures of the Land Art and Earthworks movement with familiar names (Morris, Heizer, Smithson, etc.) to the more prosaic and difficult to summarize in pithy descriptions or one or two striking images. From this period, the work of Mary Miss, Helen and Newton Mayer Harrison, Agnes Denes, or even some projects by Richard Serra (for example, Shift, 1970) particularly come to mind. The results could be inspiring or dispiriting, often both. Bruce Nauman's 1970 Amplified Tree Piece drilled a hole and inserted a microphone deep into a tree and then connected it to a speaker in a nearby room to "amplify its resonances." The tree died. (Holmes 2022, 84)

Sound and Environmental Art

Like environmental or eco-art, the study of sound is, of course, its own distinct discipline that splinters into and overlaps with a number of sub-categories based on their relation to nature. In addition to the aforementioned study of soundscapes advanced by Shafer, there are environmental sound art, acoustic ecology, eco-acoustics, ecological sound art, to name only a few. Obviously, there is overlap between many of these terms and I do not wish to dismiss the important differences between them. Instead, I will focus the remainder of this chapter on how more contemporary examples of place-based, site-specific work inform or align with Lin's Confluence Project. Like the claim made in the first chapter that every work of art is now also a work about the environment, Holmes uses a similar analogy between sound art and the environment: "Every work of sound art involves an environment." (Holmes 2022, 84) This is clear in the same way that Kaprow's "environments" became a performance of loosely scripted, defamiliarized everyday activities that blurred the boundaries between artist and viewer, or producer and consumer. As environments, happenings, and installation art began to foreground an experience of sound as material and vital experiential component as, or even more important in some cases, than vision, works began to engage the ear as much as the eye in much place-based, site-specific work.

Holmes describes several soundwalks relevant to the Confluence Project. Soundwalks are early manifestations of works that combine curated or predetermined routes and that "incorporate environmental sound as a major part of a non-musical work, outside of the concert hall." LISTEN (1966) and Times Square (1977) by Max Neuhaus, both of which took place in Manhattan, combine the ambient noises of their surroundings with directives or prompts for active listening at various locations. For LISTEN, Neuhaus invited a small group of friends to walk from a power plant on the East River to a location on the Lower East Side. "LISTEN" had been stamped on everyone's hands and Neuhaus provided no additional instructions. (Holmes 2022, 30) Times Square is often described as a low mechanical hum emanating from a grate beneath the pedestrian island in one of New York's most iconic and trafficked spaces. It was designed as a slight addition to the soundscape that would be subtly discernible to the listener eliciting a kind of "what's that?" reaction. Hildegard Westerkamp developed her own practice of soundwalks as a dedicated manner of listening to the environment. She describes herself as an acoustic ecologist while emphasizing that humans, their noises, and the sounds we associate with the natural environment coexist. Soundwalks like Queen Elizabeth Park (1974 and 2001) and A Walk Through the City (1981), performed in Toronto, utilize field recordings, maps, and interactive instructions to encourage attentive or active listening strategies unique to their surrounding contexts.

A growing number of contemporary Native American artists are also exploring sound-based site-specific work, albeit with a different perspective on time, space, habitat, and belonging. Postcommodity's Do You Remember When? was first exhibited at Arizona State University in 2009. A four-foot block of cement and marble was cut out of the floor in the gallery exposing the dirt underneath. The block was placed on a pedestal in the corner and a microphone was hung from the ceiling, dangling close to the newly exposed earth. Members of the Pee Posh and other Indigenous tribes of the region were invited to perform traditional songs. The work's confrontational title question was directed at audiences including settlers and Native visitors, prompting them to think about the associations we make between place, memory, and identity. Mark Watson writes: "In Do You Remember When?, the Indigenous sense of land is recovered and asserted, involving both a common respect for Indigenous sovereignty and an ethical focus on human–environmental reciprocity." [Watson 2015, 142] Rebecca Belmore's

Ayumee-aawach Oomama-mowan: Speaking to Their Mother (1991/1996) and Wave Sound (2017) are two works that position the land and the people who inhabit it as interlocutors. In response to the 1990 Mohawk Nation uprising against a proposed golf course expansion that would destroy a sacred grove of trees on the tribal lands of Kanetsatake, Belmore built a hand-made six-foot long megaphone and invited Indigenous speakers to talk to, and with, the land. (Davis 2021, 210) Wave Sound reversed this dynamic. Belmore was commissioned to construct four separate listening cones to be placed at national parks across Canada for the country's sesquicentennial anniversary celebration. The sculpture at Lake Superior, for example, invites visitors to listen to the surrounding birdsong and the sound of waves lapping against the shoreline. Heather Davis argues that the installation of the cones at national parks risks being absorbed by the same state-sanctioned legal structures that led to Indigenous displacement and climate change's extractive practices. But she acknowledges that the work "insists upon the land as both before and after the effects of settler colonization. In listening to the land, we are asked to listen to the deep time of the land, to its changes, and to the innumerable bodies and lives of humans and other-than-humans that have sought refuge along these shores." (Davis 2021, 211)

The work listed above is not meant to be an exhaustive survey. Certainly, there are individual sound pieces or ongoing projects from artists like Janet Cardiff or Bernie Krause that inform the Confluence Project. For example, Cardiff many soundwalks and installations are often situated at an interface between humans and human-made or manipulated environments. Mallin's Night Walk explores the forest as a keeper of secrets, unconscious desires, and fears. Bernie Krause coined the terms biophony, geophony, anthropophony, and technophony. He has been archiving the sounds of the natural world for decades. His book, The Great Animal Orchestra, a memoir of the sounds and places of his life, includes a chapter focusing on the region around Wallowa Lake, the homelands of the Nez Perce. I am also mindful of art historian Jessica Horton's suspicion of genealogies that list Native American artists after Euro-Americans or already canonized figures. ("Indigenous Artists against the Anthropocene – Whitman College" 2017, 59) This bracketing of artistic practice around identity and ethnicity risks reinscribing the very same power dynamics these artists seek to unsettle. Instead, I wish to highlight Lin's longtime investment in sound.

The sonic iconography (iconic sonography?) of Maya Lin's artistic practice is often overlooked. The Bell Tower (2011) at Shantou University in Guangdong, China is a 5000-pound bell suspended from an arcing steel support that wraps around a solid stone masonry tower. Many of the river channel and lakebed sculptures that make up her Systematic Landscapes series are fabricated from sonar renderings. But it is What is Missing? that represents Lin's most sustained use of sound as a material component of her sculptural practice. The ongoing, crowd-sourced virtual archive of species and habitat loss might best be viewed as an umbrella project that enfolds several standalone physical sculptures for which sound is a crucial component. Other works include the Listening Cone, Times Square Billboard, a two-week collaboration with the public art organization Creative Time in 2010, and the Sound Ring (2014), a large elliptical oval made of American walnut that stands seven-feet tall from base to top and nearly ten-feet across. The sculpture looks like a portal, or even an expensive, oversized hula hoop. In pictures, it seems haphazardly propped against the wall of the Cornell Laboratory of Ornithology in Ithaca, New York. This informality is part of the work's appeal, inviting curiosity and investigation for visitors drawn by the recorded sounds of birds and animals coming from tiny speakers embedded in its circumference and sourced from the laboratory where the sculpture is installed. The Listening Cone is a 20-foot long, attenuated tube made from bronze and reclaimed redwood. It sits in the east courtyard of the San Francisco Academy of Sciences and resembles a felled, hollowed tree trunk. The mouth of the cone is nearly ten-feet high. A soundtrack of bird and animal noises prompts visitors to look inside, where a small screen at the opposite end plays short videos of birds and mammals with accompanying text about climate change and disappearing biodiversity. Like the Sound Ring, the recorded animal calls and noises were donated to Lin's project from the Cornell Ornithology Lab. Compared to the Sound Ring that uses negative space to suggest emptiness, the Cone as viewed along its periphery appears like a solid, heavy object. Screen and sound compel viewers to enter the space and make their way inside, bending and stooping as they get closer to the screen. Many of the same videos that appear inside the Cone also played in New York's Times Square over a two-week period in the spring of 2010. What is Missing? videos and sound were projected over MTV's giant HD screens in Times Square to coincide with Earth Day, inserting scenes and cries of loons, whales, and geese into the visual cacophony of midtown Manhattan. Like Neuhaus's sound piece for Times Square, the goal was to create a brief moment to pause and contemplate sound and imagery that were otherwise foreign to this dense, oversaturated urban environment. Like Postcommodity's displaced concrete that allows for the earth to have its own moment to speak, Lin's work asks us to hear those sounds that we take for granted or that may soon be absent. And like Belmore's megaphones and her own listening devices that compel us to hear, speak, and act, Lin's sound work, too, asks humans to stop the harm we're doing to the environment before the species that share our world are silenced.

Ways of Listening

To this point, I have mostly stated or implied that the "we" who listen at the Bird Blind are human beings. And, of course, that is the primary intended audience at Sandy River Delta. This not only ignores the role of hearing and sound and other placemaking senses possessed by non-human species, it also universalizes a human subjectivity undifferentiated from individual experience, lived identities, and the myriad other contingencies that inform what and how people hear. Sound studies have taken up the concept of "critical listening positions" to address these issues. (Robinson 2020) Indigenous scholars and those working on Native American histories have specifically addressed "settler colonial listening positions." David Garneau states that settler colonialism is characterized by an ocular-centric worldview that *sees* nature as resources to be extracted. "The colonial attitude is characterized not only by scopophilia, a drive to look, but also by an urge to penetrate, to traverse, to know, to translate, to own and exploit … everything is ultimately comprehensible, a potential commodity, resource, or salvage." (Garneau 2016, 23) This passage accurately describes the last two-plus centuries of the American West of which Lewis and Clark's expedition is a crucial pivot point—a harbinger of a rapid, radical, and totalizing territorial displacement of older lifeways and relations to nature in the region. It also defines settler colonial attitudes toward the Columbia as extractive resource that characterizes the river to this day. Artist Leah Barclay adds that "Listening to changing environments—both in situ and through virtual experiences or creative interpretations—can evoke profound interconnection and empathetic responses that have the capacity to inspire climate action." I would argue that the Bird Blind is an effort to create such an empathetic response to the ecosystem of Sandy River Delta. It attempts to break the cycle of extractive listening (and seeing) of the settler colonial listening position. In a recent podcast interview, Lin stressed that we have seen 40–70 percent decline of songbirds over the last 50 years. "I'm actually going to try to wake you up to things that are missing that you're not even aware or disappearing," she says about this disappearing soundscape. ("Maya Lin's Memorial to Vanishing Nature" n.d., Yale 360)

There are, of course, features of the Bird Blind and Confluence in general that risk reinforcing the very same settler colonial mindset and exploitative relation to the land. While the Bird Blind is meant to be a work in relative harmony with its surroundings, it is also a structure associated with identifying, quantifying, and categorizing—practices that are important to understanding the world around us but not necessarily a world for the birds. Bird Blinds can also connote a threat of violence. The structures are arguably used more frequently for hunting than they are for bird watching. Finally, a work that commemorates the Corps of Discovery and uses their journal transcripts reproduces the very language of trade, development, and extraction that was the mission's objective. That the works are also located on state park lands and required years of coordinating with federal and state agencies, including the Army Corps of Engineers, may diminish the importance of those Indigenous histories that predate Western settlement and that Lin has sought to include. Writing about Wave Sound, Davis argues that visitors may not pick up on the "subtle and ambiguous calls to listen to the water [and that by doing so] this work resonates within the larger calls to listen to the authority of Indigenous peoples, to listen to the ways that the land and water are desperately trying to articulate the violence being done to them." The same statement might apply to the Bird Blind. Visitors may not listen or hear (or care) that so many of the animals inscribed on the slats are listed as endangered or extinct.

Jonathan Gilmurray asks the question, "What is the sound of climate change?" He lists several possibilities including the "groan and crash of calving glaciers" and the noise of the fossil fuel-burning machines present in our daily lives. He then asks readers to consider sound's absence, "the ever-decreasing variety of animal calls as species go extinct, or the silencing of the once-rich soundscapes of the earth's tropical rainforests." The current absence of birdsong and the other sounds of animals Lewis and Clark encountered and documented on their journey is ultimately unknowable. It is impossible to hear what makes no sound. Or is it? Returning to Said's concept of interpreting the soundscape contrapuntally, might silence make room to remember those histories of the dispossessed peoples and species? Can we take up Deep Listening practices to reorient our senses toward those absences, or their traces? Or can we use Deep Listening to hear the musical counterpoint between birdsong and airplanes, highways and barking dogs, to pay closer attention to those noises and emanations from the biosphere, the land, and the water, all of which are "desperately trying to articulate the violence being done to them." (Gilmurray 2016, 71)

Note

1 These include the Grand Ronde, Kalapuya, Molala, Chinook, Clackamas, Yakama, and Tualatin, in addition to those tribes who shared the vast river systems of the Willamette Valley and beyond.

References

Allan, Stacey. 2009. "Role Refusal: On Louise Lawler's Birdcalls." *Afterall: A Journal of Art, Context and Enquiry* 20 (April): 108–13. https://doi.org/10.1086/aft.20.20711738

"April 6, 1806 | Journals of the Lewis and Clark Expedition." n.d. Accessed October 1, 2023. https://lewisandclarkjournals.unl.edu/item/lc.jrn.1806-04-06#n31040613

"April 7, 1806 | Journals of the Lewis and Clark Expedition." n.d. Accessed October 10, 2023. https://lewisandclarkjournals.unl.edu/item/lc.jrn.1806-04-07

"April 13, 1806 | Journals of the Lewis and Clark Expedition." n.d. Accessed October 1, 2023. https://lewisandclarkjournals.unl.edu/item/lc.jrn.1806-04-13

Archuleta, Greg, and Jesse Norton. 2021. *Sandy River Delta Plant Inventory Report*. Prepared for the Sandy River Watershed Council.

"Confluence Project Records—Archives West." 2018. WCMss.444-2018-021. Whitman College and Northwest Archives. https://archiveswest.orbiscascade.org/ark:/80444/xv285430

Cox, Christoph, and Daniel Warner. 2004. *Audio Culture: Readings in Modern Music*. New York, NY: Continuum.

Davis, Heather. 2021. "The Breathing Land: On Questions of Climate Change and Settler Colonialism." In *The Routledge Companion to Contemporary Art, Visual Culture, and Climate Change*, 204–14.

Deloria, Vine. 2012. *Indians of the Pacific Northwest: From the Coming of the White Man to the Present Day.* Golden, CO: Fulcrum Pub.

Garneau, David. 2016. "Imaginary Spaces of Conciliation and Reconciliation: Art, Curation, and Healing."

Gilmurray, Jonathan. 2016. "Sounding the Alarm: An Introduction to Ecological Sound Art." *Muzikološki Zbornik* 52 (2): 71–84. https://doi.org/10.4312/mz.52.2.71-84

Holmes, Thom. 2022. *Sound Art: Concepts and Practices.* New York, NY: Routledge. https://doi.org/10.4324/9781315623047

"Indigenous Artists against the Anthropocene – Whitman College." 2017. Accessed October 1, 2023. https://sherlock.whitman.edu/discovery/fulldisplay?docid=cdi_proquest_journals_2172133831&context=PC&vid=01ALLIANCE_WHITC:WHITC_NEW&lang=en&search_scope=primo_central&adaptor=Primo%20Central&tab=default_all&query=any,contains,horton%20indigenous%20artists%20anthropocene&mode=Basic

Ingram, David. 2023. "The Clutter of the Unkempt Forest": John Cage, Music and American Environmental Thought."

Jacobsen, Jane, and Daniel Harkenridder. n.d. Box 9, Folder 15. Confluence Project Records.

Kaeding, Kristine M. 2010. "Monument or Folly? Maya Lin's Bird Blind at the Sandy River Delta, Oregon (2006, Confluence Project)." University of Oregon.

"Land Bridge, Five Years Old, Draws People to Crossroads, Meeting Place." 2013. The Columbian. Accessed September 26, 2023. https://www.columbian.com/news/2013/aug/24/ties-to-the-river-past-land-bridge-five-years/

Lin, Maya. 2015. *Maya Lin: Topologies.* New York, NY: Rizzoli.

"Maya Lin's Memorial to Vanishing Nature." n.d. Yale E360. Accessed October 1, 2023. https://e360.yale.edu/features/maya_lin_a_memorial_to_a_vanishing_natural_world

Nesbit, Sharon. 2007. *It Could Have Been Carpdale: Centennial History of Troutdale, Oregon, 1907–2007.* Battle Ground, WA: Pediment Publishing.

Nisbet, James. 2014. *Ecologies, Environments, and Energy Systems in Art of the 1960s and 1970s.* Cambridge, MA: The MIT Press.

Robinson, Dylan. 2020. "Hungry Listening: Resonant Theory for Indigenous Sound Studies." In *Indigenous Americas.* Minneapolis, MN: University of Minnesota Press.

Said, Edward W. 1993. *Culture and Imperialism.* New York, NY: Knopf.

"Sandy River." n.d. Accessed September 23, 2023. https://www.nwcouncil.org/reports/columbia-river-history/sandyriver/

"Study of H5N1 Avian Flu Seal Deaths Reveals Multiple Lineages | CIDRAP." 2023. Accessed March 15, 2023. https://www.cidrap.umn.edu/avian-influenza-bird-flu/study-h5n1-avian-flu-seal-deaths-reveals-multiple-lineages

Sturken, Marita. 1991. "The Wall, the Screen, and the Image: The Vietnam Veterans Memorial." *Representations* 35: 118–42. https://doi.org/10.2307/2928719

Weston, Phoebe. 2022. "Half of World's Bird Species in Decline as Destruction of Avian Life Intensifies." *The Guardian*, September 28, 2022, sec. Environment. https://www.theguardian.com/environment/2022/sep/28/nearly-half-worlds-bird-species-in-decline-as-destruction-of-avian-life-intensifies-aoe

4   The Story Circles of Sacajawea State Park

Race, Ethnicity, Confluence

During an episode of the podcast *What It Takes* posted in 2018, Maya Lin was interviewed about how her upbringing informs her artistic and architectural practice. Lin was born in Athens, Ohio, and she lived surrounded by vibrant creativity. Her mother, Julia Chang Lin, was a poet and literature professor at Ohio University. Her father, Henry Huan Lin, was a well-known ceramicist and dean of the College of Fine Arts on the same campus. Lin's father immigrated to the United States in 1948, and her mother came the following year during a period of immense turmoil in China that culminated in October with Chairman Mao's proclamation of the founding of the People's Republic of China. When Lin was born a decade later, her parents had already established academic careers and worked to assimilate their children (Lin's brother, Tan Lin, is a well-known poet) into American society, a goal broadly shared by many of that generation's immigrant families. For her parents, this meant adopting many mid-Western customs and immersing the children in the English language. During the interview, Lin makes a startling statement about her awareness of her own racial and ethnic identity as a young girl, an observation worth quoting at length:

> Growing up, I thought I was White. Didn't occur to me that I wasn't White. I'm very mid-Western in a lot of my affectations, what I like to eat. It probably didn't occur to me I was Asian-American until I was studying abroad in Denmark actually and there was a little bit of prejudice, racial discrimination, because as I get a suntan I look like a Greenlander. And as the US had a certain prejudice against Native Americans, the Danes had a similar read towards the Greenlanders. And all of a sudden, they would be moving away from me on the bus. They wouldn't sit next to me. There would be these weird comments. And growing up, I think I was very, I would say naïve. Our home life was very, very close-knit. It was my mother, my father, my brother and I. I never knew my grandparents on either side. When I was very little, we would get letters and they'd be censored, from China,

DOI: 10.4324/9781003309024-5

in Chinese. So we were a very insular little family. We stayed very close to home. I think that's Chinese?

("Maya Lin: The Art of Remembrance" 2018)

Lin has spoken candidly elsewhere about her ethnic background prior to this podcast, perhaps most poignantly in the Bill Moyers documentary *Becoming an American: The Chinese Experience* first broadcast in 2003. The Academy Award-winning documentary about the making of the Vietnam Veteran's Memorial, *Maya Lin: A Strong Clear Vision*, also includes ugly instances of racism directed at Lin during the public hearings prior to the work's completion. Her statement here—"Growing up, I thought I was White,"—is a fascinating disclosure. Why would Lin think she was White; or, more importantly, why would it matter if Lin thought she was White? This racial misrecognition provides an opportunity to address how the roles of race, ethnicity, and the politics of identity have shaped the Confluence Project.

There was initial backlash to Lin's involvement coming from within Native American communities. Why was an Asian-American artist from Ohio chosen to oversee a work dealing with Indigenous peoples and cultures of the Northwest Plateau? Were there no Native American artists more appropriate for the project? The issue was pronounced enough for Roberta Conner (Confederated Tribes of the Umatilla Indian Reservation, CTUIR) to address it in a talk at the 2012 American Association of Museums annual meeting: "We had to defend why it wasn't a tribal artist." (Confluence Project Records—Archives West" 2018, Box 1, Folder 4) The involvement of respected tribal leaders like Conner, Minthorn, Ray Gardner (Chinook), Johnpaul Jones, Wilfrid Scott, and Horace Axtell (Nez Perce) and many others from the earliest stages of Confluence's development no doubt tempered this backlash. Nevertheless, Lin's involvement is an opportunity to consider how the dynamics of race and ethnicity operate within the Confluence Project, specifically at Sacajawea State Park.

Art: Story Circles

The Confluence artworks at Sacajawea State Park were dedicated in 2010. The Corps of Discovery briefly camped where the Snake and Columbia Rivers meet from October 16–18, 1805. Maya Lin foregrounds Native American customs and rituals at this site through the construction of seven discreet "Story Circles," a series of earthworks clustered in a grassy area at the southwestern edge of the park. Made from sculpted, three-foot-tall basalt blocks approximately affixed to one another with stainless steel joints. Some circles are sunken into the earth, while others rise above the ground. Each varies in circumference with the largest approximately 20 feet across and the smallest around ten feet. This arrangement and variation creates an inviting topography

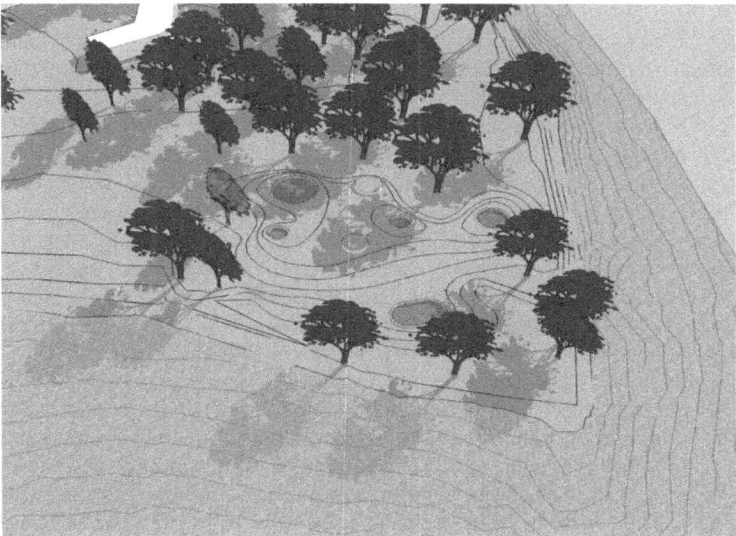

Figure 4.1 Computer rendering of the peninsula and seven Story Circles, Jones & Jones Architects and Landscape Architects, ca. 2005.

Sources: Box 7, Folders 43–44. WCMss444. Confluence Project Records. Whitman College and Northwest Archives.

barely discernible until viewers are up-close. The circles are bounded by the Snake River to the East, the Columbia to the southwest, a small recreational beach to the south, the WPA-era Sacajawea Museum, and a lagoon and boat dock to the north Figure 4.1. An interpretive trail and timeline featuring metal placards with didactic text mounted on steel poles run along a paved pathway by the park's Snake River side.

Each circle has its own theme: Welcome, Rivers, Tribes, Trade, Coyote, Salmon, and Seasonal Rounds. Expository text is sandblasted onto the basalt fragments around the exterior or interior perimeter of every enclosure. For example, the Welcome Circle rises above ground, and text carved into its exterior explains the significance of the location to Native peoples and notes the dates of the Corp's encampment. While the Welcome Circle is typically the first installation encountered by visitors, because of its proximity to the museum and parking lot, the circles are not intended to be experienced in a particular order. This feature encourages exploration, contemplation, and a holistic, phenomenological encounter with the art, echoing the design program of the other sites. There is no single order in which to view the circles and their arrangement eschews linear, hierarchical patterns of Euro-American epistemologies.

The Seasonal Rounds Circle sits nearby, its much larger footprint is necessary to accommodate the comprehensive names and images of flora and fauna listed on the interior of the enclosure. In contrast to the Welcome Circle, this one is sunken into the ground. The Seasonal Round is a description of the foods that formed the dietary foundation of tribes east of the Cascades and Celilo Falls. Explanatory text—"Columbia Plateau peoples followed the seasons, gathering, hunting and fishing according to the annual cycle"—is engraved over icons of mussels, steelhead, spring and fall chinook salmon, silver salmon, sage grouse, pacific lamprey, and mule deer. The animals are situated alongside images of bitterroot, bulrush, Indian hemp, chokecherry, wild onion, and two varieties of balsamroot. (A complete list can be found at Confluence's website.) The Sahaptin terms for the seasons are listed above the icons and identifiers alongside the English translation: "anim WINTER | wawaxam SPRING | satim SUMMER | spam FALL". Often labeled "First Foods," the Seasonal Round also refers to the communal practice of gathering those same foods and the importance of this location as a source of exchange between river tribes and plains Indians.

The significance of the use of Sahaptin terms to identify the different times of year should not be overlooked. Indian dispossession of lands was coupled with forced or coerced relocation to reservations, and the removal of children to abusive boarding schools where they were not allowed to speak their own language. Erasure of language and culture are the strategies of genocide and extermination. The translations were a result of collaboration with the CTUIR: … and Dr. Virginia Beavert, a member of the Yakama Nation and a teacher at the University of Oregon's Northwest Indian Language Institute, who have worked diligently to recover and preserve Sahaptin. Acknowledging Indigenous terminology is an important step in recognizing tribal sovereignty and confronting the horrors of physical and cultural violence against Native Americans. (Hunn 2015)

To the immediate west of the Seasonal Round Circle and facing the Columbia are the Rivers Circle and Coyote Circle. The former, also called "rivers before dams," emphasizes the crucial role of the site for thousands of years prior to settler colonial contact. It describes how the actual "river bank that had supported tremendous cultural and ecological activity was submerged" by construction of the McNary Dam in 1953. The latter tells the story of Coyote, the mythical trickster central to Indigenous folklore, who gifted salmon to people, telling them "Every year they will come up this river." The text is taken from a traditional Yakama and Klickitat tale. The two circles' installation side-by-side near the Columbia's banks is a poignant juxtaposition. Coyote's gift to all peoples is squandered by the damming of the river over the past 70 years. The words of the Rivers circle offer a subtle rebuke to the fetishization of the Lewis and Clark expedition by stating that the actual location of their encampment is submerged. Finding the exact spot where members of the Corps of Discovery walked, hunted, ate, and slept is an obsession for trail and expedition connoisseurs. While the erasure of Indigenous histories is vastly more profound, inundation of the landscape for irrigation and energy obscures more recent pasts as well.

The Trade Circle is perched above ground in close proximity to the beach. This and the Tribes Circle are closest to the tip of the peninsula, where the two rivers meet. Descriptive text is inscribed underneath the items, noting that the site has been utilized "for more than 10,000 years" and has welcomed Native people from the coast to the Rocky Mountains who traveled by foot, water, and later horseback. Each basalt segment is inscribed with an important article of exchange carved on the exterior of the enclosure near the top of the block. Like the Seasonal Round, Sahaptin terms are used, followed by their English translation. "| qixli TULE MATS | calamat STONE PIPES | axsaxs DENTALIUM | tawax TOBACCO | lucali COPPER | yapaas SALMON OIL | mixsli BRASS | wapaas WOVEN BAGS | anps BASKETS | satay WOOL BLANKETS | wasimtatsay BISON ROBES | sapincaas PIGMENTS | waltaki SALMON PEMMICAN | cimcim GLASS BEADS | cuksh OBSIDIAN | xapilmi STEEL KNIVES | lat'ixw GUNPOWDER |". I include the full list here because it emphasizes the complexity of Native American cultures for audiences that have become conditioned to flattened, one-dimensional images of Indian life fed to us through mass media and popular culture. These terms are not just words for specific materials vital to Plateau and Coastal inhabitants. They are descriptors of a vast way of life, economies of exchange that denote geography, habitat, custom, ritual, and interpersonal dynamics. Tule mats, for example, are woven panels made from thick, durable sedge grasses. They expand and contract depending on weather conditions and were used in many contexts, but were most commonly stacked and hung over one another to create longhouse walls. Dentalium, or the tusks, teeth, or shells from large animals, were used for ornamentation and displays of wealth but were also practical carving tools. This list also recognizes manufactured items that preceded Lewis and Clark's expedition. Steel, gunpowder, brass, and wool were products of Western colonial cultures and were exchanged for access to territories coveted by fur trappers well before the Corps of Discovery's journey.

The Salmon Circle is dedicated to the only species represented in more than one circle, symbolizing its immense importance to life on or near the Columbia River. "tkw'nat" is the Chinook term for salmon; "susayns" means steelhead. "kalux" is the Sahaptin term for sockeye, and "sinux" is silver salmon. "ascins" refers to bull trout. Images of the different sub-species are, like the text, sandblasted into the basalt blocks. Like the Trade circle, didactic text is carved underneath the Sahaptin words, their English counterparts, and the accompanying icons, reminding viewers that salmon migrated by the millions upriver every year for eons to spawn at this point. "By 2008," the text states, "each of these species was listed as threatened or endangered in one or both rivers."

The technique of sandblasting to carve the text is, of course, a modern one. But the incorporation of iconic images of flora and fauna echoes the rich history of petroglyphs and pictographs, some many thousands of years old, found on rock formations in the canyons in and around the Columbia and Snake. Ancient imagery found nearby is adapted by contemporary Native American

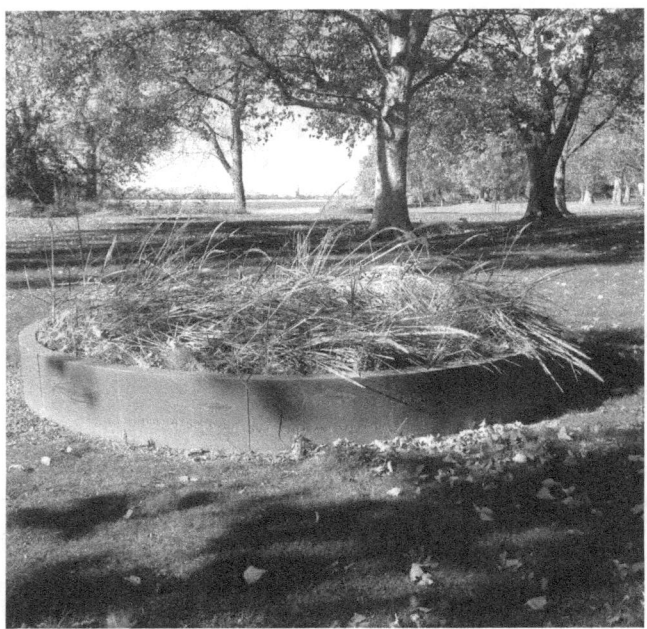

Figure 4.2 Salmon Story Circle, 2015.
Source: Photo by author.

artists and incorporated into several Confluence installations previously described. Here, the modern, more conventional salmon iconography found in the story circles acknowledges the incalculable value of salmon to Indigenous peoples as well as the present moment of habitat loss. It also pleads for a future in which salmon might be restored to the river. Writing about the "fish wars" of the nineteenth and twentieth centuries and Native sovereignty, Emily Washines (Yakama) narrates the long history of promises to maintain treaty rights to those fishing locations used by Indians since "time immemorial." Such promises were repeatedly made and repeatedly broken by local and state officials and the federal government. Overfishing, canneries, and dams destroyed a resource described by U.S. Supreme Court Justice Joseph McKenna in 1905 as "not much less necessary to the Indians than the atmosphere they breathed." (Hart 2022, 24) Washines reasserts the importance of sovereignty in her essay when she quotes Chief George Meninock of the Yakama Nation: "For I say to you that our health is from the fish; our strength is from the fish, our very life is from the fish."(Hart 2022, 27) The salmon circle rises up from the ground Figure 4.2. When salmon return to the river and thrive again, it will be because of efforts made by Indians to keep them alive.

The final circle to be described here is, in fact, not a circle at all but an elliptical enclosure that mimics the footprint of a native longhouse, a social and ceremonial space central to the cultural traditions of the Indigenous tribes along the Columbia. Longhouses were multifamily, multipurpose structures, used primarily as dwellings during the winter. Exteriors were composed of the aforementioned tule mats hung from tall, sturdy, skinny poles that allowed for relatively easy construction and disassembly during warmer seasons. Archival records initially described this as the dwelling circle, framing it as an introduction to the site. ("Confluence Project Records—Archives West" 2018, Box 7, Folder 43) It is positioned, however, at the southeasternmost tip of the park. This might make an awkward starting point for contemporary viewers coming from the parking lot until you remember that for millennia, the vast majority of visitors to this location would have entered via canoe from either river. Text sandblasted onto the exterior of the circle states that the site is near the ancient village of Kw'sis, home to "region's Sahaptin-speaking people [who] gathered to fish, trade, and hold ceremonies." Text etched into the interior of the same circle using the same technique lists those tribes associated with the area: "Walla Walla, Palouse, Palus, Yakama, Wanapam, Cayuse, Umatilla, Nez Perce." The symbolic importance of listing the tribes on the interior reinforces the concept that the park is only a few decades old, while tribal histories at this location extend much further back in time.

"Maya's Suggestion": Plans and Interpretation

When encountered from a distance, the circles blend into the scenery. The sunken earthworks are barely discernible, often eliciting a kind of "is that all there is?" reaction from the students and friends with whom I have visited the site. While this might be an effective technique for encouraging viewers to look harder, this was not the original design plan. Archival documents demonstrate an evolving, at times difficult, process of negotiation between Lin, John Paul Jones, and the numerous local and state agencies involved. A topographical map of the park from 2003 (double check) overlaid with hand-drawn sketches and labeled "Maya's suggestion" illustrates an initial brainstorm of possibilities. These included a reworked portage dock in the northwest lagoon, a site frequently used by local fishermen and recreational boaters. Vegetation surrounding the dock would be restored to native varietals. An interpretive trail along the Snake shoreline would be enhanced, and "teaching stations" would be situated at smaller riverside piers. A larger "gathering ring" would be installed at the southernmost tip of the park and tell the story of the Seasonal Round and salmon. An introductory ring would abut the rear of the museum. The proposal's plan for a small plaza situated at the vertex between the two wings of the historic building would have created a more inviting entry point from the parking lot. Handwritten notes on the Columbia side of the plan indicate a desire to "make beach more natural." ("Confluence Project Records—Archives West" 2018, Box 7, Folder 43)

The aforementioned document was produced by Maya Lin Studios and, although undated, appears to be one of the earliest plans for Sacajawea State Park in Whitman's archives. A more comprehensive plan that incorporated Lin's ideas was drafted by Jones & Jones and submitted for commentary and revision to the various state park constituencies in early 2005, along with tribes and other stakeholder groups, including the Nez Perce, the CTUIR, and the Yakama Nation, along with members of the U.S. Army Corp of Engineers, all of whom suggested or required significant changes. Lin was particularly interested in the lagoon, noting its circular boundary, proximity to the ancient Indian village, and a desire to salvage a working portage boat dock. The latter would have created a usable piece of infrastructure for fishing and recreation. Notes taken at the site and labeled "Maya's Suggestion" stressed a desire to pursue these improvements "from an aesthetic viewpoint." ("Confluence Project Records—Archives West" 2018, Box 8, Folder 1) Lin and Jones collaborated on proposed different dock designs, all of which would have used quotes from the Lewis and Clark journals that describe the point's features embedded or carved into a steel boardwalk, similar to the use of passages from the journals at other sites. Memos and emails from Washington State Parks personnel were diplomatic in response to these ideas. On the one hand, they supported Lin's ideas and her work at Sacajawea. On the other hand, it was their job to alert her to aspects of the plan that might be too burdensome or expensive to complete. Parks staff pointed out the complexity of acquiring permits to build on water, the delicate archeological sensitivity of any construction, the Wanapum tribe's own interest in honoring the ancient village at a future date, a separate plan for expansion of the museum, and concern for the other historic structures and markers at the park.

Time and money were also starting to play more prominent factors in the execution of the remaining sites. By fall of 2005, when a revised proposal was drafted, it was clear that the seven physical installations would not be completed before the end of the Lewis and Clark bicentennial. Estimates for Sacajawea State Park in early budgets allocated $900,000 in 2003 for the site. ("Confluence Project Records – Archives West" n.d., Box 1, Folder 25) Even after built-in contingency spending was accounted for, that number had grown to well over $1 million before any on-site work began. ("Confluence Project Records—Archives West" 2018, Box 7, Folder 10) Confluence had been raising private funds and applying for grants from the outset, but archival records show a renewed emphasis on offsetting rising costs through private benefactors. Administrative records from this period show vigorous fiscal development efforts, including spreadsheets with hundreds of possible donors and points of contact, lists of private and public arts foundations, and payments to consultants and other independent contractors for assistance in these efforts. A handwritten administrative meeting note from around this period stated in all caps: "NEED: MONEY, PUBLICITY, BIG TIME SUPPORT." A doodle on a facing page showed a single solitary stick-figure pulling the bow of a giant ship. ("Confluence Project Records—Archives West" 2018, Box 8, Folder 10) Conflicts also arose between the infrastructural needs of the state parks system and the Confluence design team's creative aspirations. An email exchange between state parks managers and consulting architects at Jones & Jones is illustrative of the kinds of negotiations taking place under a compressed timeline and tightening budget. "The Confluence Project's primary focus is on the Maya Lin Artworks and shoreline restoration, not on facility improvements," Jones & Jones wrote to the Washington State Parks Eastern Region office in response to suggested improvements. "CP is in the challenging position of raising funds and jumping the permitting hoop for the project elements we've already committed to. While WA State Parks and other agencies may offer wonderful suggestions for even greater improvements, the reality is that our client's budget and project scope are already tough enough to achieve within the compressed timeline." ("Confluence Project Records—Archives West" 2018, Box 8, Folder 6)

Ironically, some of the proposed artistic concepts would have benefitted the long-term health of the riverine and ecological systems at the expense of the shorter-term use of both rivers as extractive resources. Plans for comprehensive shoreline restoration, reestablishment of native vegetation, and construction of a breach berm between the lagoon and Snake River were attempts to rebuild more sustainable ecological habitats for fish and wildlife. While such efforts were realized, their ambitions had to be dramatically scaled back. Proposed artistic concepts faced additional obstacles over adherence to the park's historical preservation requirements. Non-native trees and landscaping, the WPA-era museum, and a marker dedicated to the park's founders, the Daughters of the Pioneers, were all historical structures that fell under federal and state preservation guidelines. Washington State Parks had always planned to upgrade the museum facility. Lin's ideas would have better integrated the Confluence Project with the building, but it is likely those renovations were themselves already in motion. There is little in the archival record about the museum renovation.

The most ambitious element during these early planning stages was a large, elevated earthwork mound near the current location of the Seasonal Rounds circle Figure 4.3. Described variously as "Maya's Compass Circle," "Native Peoples Round," and "Homeland Geography" earthwork, the proposal called for a series of three concentric circles several feet above the ground. The exterior circle would be approximately 100 feet in diameter with three-to-four entryways facing the Columbia, Snake, and southernmost point of the park where the rivers meet. A middle circle 50 feet in diameter would have a single opening on the northern side leading to the smallest, interior circle. This last enclosure is described in a portfolio of multiple plans as banked higher on its northern end, sloping toward the southern tip to "allow a strong visual connection to the water." ("Confluence Project Records—Archives West" 2018, Box 8, Folder 4) The result would have required visitors to walk around the interior rims of each circle, much like a mandala or labyrinth. The provisional descriptions in these earlier plans indicate an evolving process, but they advanced far enough for Lin to create a series of compelling drawings and for

Jones & Jones to develop more detailed illustrations. Lin also molded a clay maquette of the compass earthwork design that was used in the Henry Art Gallery's exhibition Systematic Landscapes in 2006. ("Confluence Project Records—Archives West" 2018, Object 6)

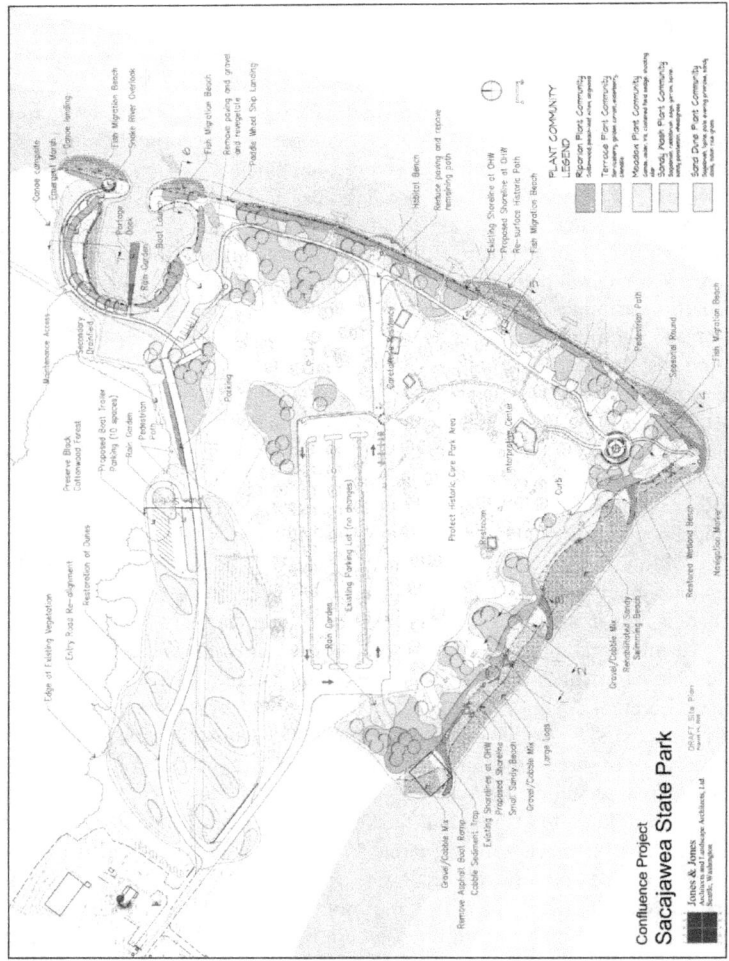

Figure 4.3 Draft Site Plan for Sacajawea State Park, Jones & Jones Architects and Landscape Architects, August 14, 2006.

Sources: Box 8, Folder 4. WCMss444. Confluence Project Records. Whitman College and Northwest Archives.

It would be easy to dismiss the above alterations to earlier plans as compromises that diminished the aesthetic impact or undermined Lin's own environmental concerns. Those anecdotal reactions to the Story Circles seem to reinforce this observation. However, Lin and the Confluence design team had always worked under the condition that their ideas would have to be revised and approved by state and federal agencies. The primary goal of the Confluence sites has always been pedagogical. During the tense back-and-forth between Jones & Jones and Washington State Parks, the parties managed to find common ground over this issue: "Confluence Project enhancements at the park are merely the catalyst for many more positive environmental and cultural changes that occur on-site over time. We hope that the projects at each of the Confluence sites will inspire and set off a movement toward creating healthy environments at Columbia River legacy sites." The archival nature of the works themselves, at Sacajawea and every location, reframes each site within a more expansive timeframe, reminding viewers of the relatively brief period of human habitation and the longer geologic and biological forces that shape place over vast eons. "What's important is that a dialogue has begun," added a park administrator in reply to frustrations expressed by the Confluence team. ("Confluence Project Records—Archives West" 2018, Box 8, Folder 6)

The Story Circles and other interpretive features and improvements ultimately completed at Sacajawea State Park are subtly effective for those who take the time to enter into conversation with the artwork. As with every Confluence location, experiencing the work in situ requires an engagement not only with the circles themselves but also with the surrounding park, the infrastructure and industry in close proximity, and the damaged ecology of both rivers. To read about the dams in the Rivers Circle is to recognize the water's controlled placidity. Navigating the circles requires a pilgrimage of sorts that circulates viewers through and around the edge of the park. For those circles with interior text, visitors might kneel or crouch down. (The location requires ADA compliance and is accessible, although this feature would obviously frustrate some disabled people.) Stooping, leaning, turning, looking up and down, and moving one's body in slow, repetitive, ritualistic fashion is the best way to encounter Sacajawea's installation. Every experience is arguably an embodied one; what makes the Story Circles unique is the manner in which it asks viewers to be conscious of the connection between corporeality and environment.

Uneasy Juxtapositions: Race, the Anthropocene, and Context at Sacajawea State Park

The compromises made to reconcile the state park's bureaucratic requirements and the creative concepts initially advocated by the Confluence design team raise a more provocative interpretation. From the early design proposals that sought a more deliberate integration between interpretive trails, outlooks, a larger story circle, and the museum to the end result in which the circles are clustered within a narrow strip of the park, yet can also appear scattered within that same space, yields uncomfortable analogies to the practice of allotment. A document in the Whitman Archives entitled "Story Circles: Tribal Lore and Archeology" prepared for research in advance of the installation's production discusses the issue of allotment and its devastating effects on Native American life. ("Confluence Project Records—Archives West" 2018, Box 8, Folder 43) In 1887, the U.S. Government passed the Dawes Act under the guise of assimilating Indians into mainstream (White) society. Also known as the "Allotment Act," the new law abrogated collective tribal authority over reservation territory and instead platted the land within reservation boundaries, giving it to Indian individuals or families, usually in 80–160-acre lots. The stated intention of the Act, beyond assimilation, was to acclimate Native Americans to property ownership and farming, "proper" uses of the land according to European-influenced conventions.

Reservation treaties of the mid-nineteenth century were honored until the land became desirable to Whites, which occurred almost immediately after those same treaties were negotiated. Furs, gold, fish, timber, farmland, water, oil, aluminum, and uranium provide just a short list of some of the material resources that could be found on reservation lands or which Indian lands stood in the way of. Eventually, individual ownership allowed some Indians to lease their lands to mining companies or non-Indian individuals in a better position to exploit their resources, a practice that became widespread. The phenomenon of smaller parcels of land dispersed within the larger territories of the reservation became known as "checkerboarding" to describe the appearance of Indian vs. non-Indian plots when viewed on a map. From a strictly formal perspective, the Story Circles disrupt the rigid, grid-like geometry of platted properties. Within the larger context of the Sacajawea State Park, however, it can bring to mind the uneasy juxtapositions between the circles and, for example, the Daughters of the Pioneers marker situated between the museum and the circle in closest proximity. The four-foot-tall monument resembles a tombstone and frames a plaque reminding visitors of the organization's gift of the park to the public. Video footage featuring Lin walking the site contains a telling moment. "This is a thing that must go away. I couldn't get it moved. I still think we should try to get that thing forcibly removed. It just shouldn't be there," she says while walking with an assistant through the construction area. ("Confluence Project Records—Archives West" 2018, 2018-021-003)

Sacajawea State Park was founded by the Daughters of the Pioneers, an all-female civic volunteer organization. Originally named the Native Daughters of the Washington State Pioneers, the group was "open to all 'native born daughters and granddaughters of white parents who were residents on the Pacific Coast prior to 1870.'" (Kubik 2001) The Pasco chapter was founded in 1926, and when the group came into possession of an acre of land at the confluence of the Snake and Columbia Rivers, they worked diligently to cultivate the site with new plantings and trees. It was donated to the city five years later. The group's charter was active in developing the site as a state park commemorating Sacajawea and the Lewis and Clark expedition.

The decision to name the park after Sacajawea was part of a larger cultural fascination that coincided with the first bicentennial of the Lewis and Clark expedition as well as First Wave feminist movements in the early part of the twentieth century that looked to heroic, accomplished female figures to hold up as models of achievement. Historians generally agree that Sacajawea was born in 1788 and affiliated with Lemhi and Shoshone tribes outside of present-day Salmon, Idaho. When she was 12 years old, she was kidnapped in a raid on her encampment by members of the Hidatsa tribe, who later sold her to Toussaint Charbonneau, a French-Canadian fur trapper. In 1804, Charbonneau took her to live at Fort Mandan in what is now North Dakota, where Lewis and Clark had camped during the first winter of their expedition. Charbonneau was hired on as a translator by the expedition, and Sacajawea joined the crew despite having recently given birth to a boy named Jean Baptiste, also called Pomp. Her role in the voyage is variously described as translator, interpreter, guide, and envoy. There is no doubt that Lewis and Clark valued her contributions immensely, and she was rewarded by them for her efforts. (Clark adopted Jean-Baptiste and his younger sister, Lisette, after Sacajawea's death and later paid for the boy's education in St. Louis.) A chance encounter with her brother Cameahwait in Shoshone territory during the Corps' westward phase likely saved the expedition from attack. Vine Deloria, Jr. goes so far as to state that without Sacajawea, the expedition would likely have failed. (Josephy and Jaffe 2006, 112) But it is also fair to say that her participation in one of the nation's founding events was not by choice. Charbonneau was known to physically abuse her, and she is often referred to as a "captive" in much of the literature on the expedition. She is thought to have died in 1812 at the age of 24 due to complications from childbirth, although based on oral history accounts, others have argued she lived nearly a century, dying in 1884. (Brooks 2004)

Charbonneau's marriage to Sacajawea highlights practices of slavery and intermarriage common to many Indian cultures. The Confluence sites west of Celilo Falls were known as slave markets. East of what is now The Dalles, slavery was practiced less frequently. Eugene Hunn speculates that the difficult climate, sparse vegetation, and fewer trees east of the Cascades promoted stronger alliances through kinship and exogamy. Where food and shelter were more difficult to obtain, cooperation and extended communities became essential to survival. [Note, 24?] When the fur trade began and French trappers migrated from Canadian provinces throughout the mountainous regions of North America, they adopted exogamy as a means to better navigate uncharted territories, out of loneliness and isolation, and as way to advance their business interests. Sacajawea and Charbonneau's children were the result of an incredibly complex mixture of ethnicities. Jean-Baptiste and his younger sibling, Lisette, were taken in by Clark in St. Louis after Sacajawea's death. (The historical record is vague about the exact circumstances of Sacajawea's death.) Jean-Baptiste lived a colorful life. He traveled in Europe, learning multiple languages, became a fur trapper, a magistrate in California prior to statehood, and a gold miner before dying of unknown causes in Danner, Oregon, in 1866. It is thought that Lisette died around her third birthday under the care of Clark.

Was Jean-Baptiste Indian? If so, what tribes might claim him? Was he French, French-Canadian, or Métis, as the intermixing of Indigenous groups and French trappers came to be known? Race, ethnicity, and nationality are not equivalent. Arguably, Jean-Baptiste is that most paradigmatic kind of American—a polyglot of ethnic backgrounds impossible to disentangle from one another. Between 1806 and the early twentieth century, bogus racial science attempted to "make race visible" by defining blood quantum into law. (Hyde 2022, 327) Historian Anne Hyde traces the history of intermarriage as a much more common, even ubiquitous, practice in settler colonial-era Western territories through the genealogy of Thomas McKay. McKay's father, Alexander, oversaw construction of Fort Astoria and was an instrumental figure in the burgeoning fur trapping business in the Pacific Northwest. His mother was Marguerite Waddens McKay, the daughter of an Ojibwa woman and Swiss fur trader. (Following Alexander's death, Mary would wed John McLoughlin, Chief Factor and Superintendent of the Hudson Bay Company at Fort Vancouver.) McKay fathered eleven children with three separate women, all of Native and European descent. Those children and their families were ultimately forced to choose between bifurcated identity categories, either assimilating into White society or embracing an Indian identity on the reservations. (Hyde 2022, 235) His three half-Chinook sons from his first marriage "became allotted Indians. Their children and grandchildren stayed near reservations, marrying Native people." His son George, born of Cree and French descent, was identified as "Indian" on his World War I draft card but recorded as White in the 1860 census. The next generation of McKay grandchildren moved from the reservation (Umatilla) to the city (Portland) and were categorized as White on future census rolls. (Hyde 2022, 329)

A place-based analysis of the landscape where the Snake and Columbia Rivers meet provides a disturbingly concentrated case study for how racial formations and the Anthropocene are deeply interwoven. Historian Blaine Harden wrote about this landscape nearly two decades ago, describing the site where Lewis and Clark first encountered the Columbia River. He characterizes it as surrounded by "agro-industrial sprawl from Pasco, Kennewick, and Richland, the towns in southeastern Washington that call themselves the Tri-Cities." He documents Chevron's massive tank farm where fossil fuels are stored, awaiting transport via barge to the larger metro areas further west, Cargill's cluster of grain elevators, the high-voltage power lines that criss-cross the river, and the "sanitary lagoons" located just west of the entrance to Sacajawea State Park. (Harden 2012, 72–73) Elsewhere, the author references the Hanford nuclear reactors, where the plutonium for the atomic bomb dropped over Nagasaki was refined as part of the Manhattan Project during

World War II. The reactors were converted to provide energy throughout the Northwest after the war. Now decommissioned, they also left behind radioactive waste stored in outmoded, leaky containers perilously close to the river's shores. Geographer Kathryn Yusoff describes how the nuclear industry "exploited and polluted Native American lands and bodies," first by stealing and decimating their ancient homelands for mining and bomb testing; later by leaving behind irradiated landscapes that poisoned poor and Native communities indefinitely. (Harden 2012, 50)

Harden's list is abbreviated, and new industrial infrastructure has steadily grown since his book's publication. This includes a giant new Amazon "fulfillment center" which serves as a regional hub for the company's ground shipping, one of North America's largest slaughterhouses, and the nearby Boise-Cascade paper mill perched on the riverbank less than ten miles from the Story Circles. The origin point for this legacy begins with the town of Ainsworth, where state park now stands. The town took its name from John Ainsworth, who ran the Oregon Steam Navigation Company. The location was a junction for the Northern Pacific Rail Road's Pend Orielle line connecting Minnesota to Eastern Washington. Surveyors began planning a townsite in 1879 where the Snake and Columbia Rivers meet and by the following year the town was home to an equal population of European and Chinese immigrant laborers. The role of Chinese men and women in the construction of North America's railroads is well-known. Ainsworth attracted laborers from cities like Portland and San Francisco, as well as the gold mines of Idaho and Montana. Ainsworth's Chinese population constantly fluctuated as workers were given seasonal contracts, or left to work at the salmon canneries. Estimates vary widely, but it is generally thought that there were anywhere from several hundred to possibly a thousand Chinese laborers in and around Ainsworth during peak work seasons. In addition, Chinese businesses (including brothels and opium dens) were so common in the town that they gained a nickname as "Chinese Ainsworth." (Meyer 1983, 14) Racial tensions often flared between the different groups. White workers concerned that cheaper wages paid to Chinese would displace them from their jobs led to many violent conflicts. In 1882, Congress passed the Chinese Exclusion Act that prevented new immigration and no longer allowed acquisition of citizenship, even for those born in the United States. The law had the added effect of unofficially sanctioning violence against Chinese communities to massacres across the country. In one case, 34 miners working in a gold mine claim near the Snake in Idaho were slaughtered by White thieves. Less than ten years after Ainsworth's construction, the railroad hub was moved across the river to Pasco, the town was abandoned, and its history was largely forgotten.

These racial configurations extend even further back in time—or perhaps it is more accurate to say that our present racial formations miscolor and poison the ancient past. The remains of what came to be called "Kennewick Man" were discovered in 1996, just upriver from Sacajawea State

Park. The body was examined by an archeological consultant, shared with a local coroner, analyzed by a forensic scientific lab, taken and locked away by the U.S. Army Corps of Engineers, and finally repatriated by an alliance of regional tribes and reburied near its ancestral homelands. In the 16 years between the skeleton's discovery and its repatriation, a debate raged over the origin and ethnicity of Kennewick Man. The skeletal remains were immediately politicized. Chatters labeled him "Caucasoid," a possible descendent of European ancestry that, if proven, could undermine Native American claims of sovereignty and rewrite thousands of years of historical claims about prehistoric cross-continental migration. Civic leaders from the nearby Tri-Cities proposed that he be renamed "Kennewick-Pasco-Richland Man." This was an outrage to Umatilla tribal leaders who insisted on the name "Oyt.pa.ma.na.tit.tite" or "The Ancient One." Eventually, the Army Corps of Engineers followed the guidelines of the Native American Graves and Repatriation Act (NAGPRA) and turned over the remains to the CTUIR for burial.

Kennewick lies only a few miles west of Sacajawea State Park, just outside the city of Pasco. Richland is just north of Kennewick and was built overnight to house the engineers and scientists working at Hanford. Kennewick Man/Oyt.pa.ma.na.tit.tite was found only a few miles downriver from Sacajawea State Park. The river junction that forms this place was a sacred gathering spot for Native Americans for millennia. When White settlers came, they saw a barren landscape devoid of trees and wildlife, a tabula rasa that would soon become a central node in the development of the location as a source and transit hub for ever-increasing resource extraction. The tug-of-war between scientists eager to study the location and Native Americans who claimed it as sacred ground ended when the Army Corps of Engineers played out along ethnic lines. An early facial reconstruction made global news due to its resemblance to the British actor Patrick Stewart from *Star Trek: The Next Generation*. After a University of Chicago study confirmed a genetic connection to Native Plateau peoples, a new model was sculpted, resembling an Ainu man Indigenous to ancient Japan. (Bulls 2018) This unique location, now home to the Confluence Project's Story Circles is densely layered with history and meaning. Decisions about the ethnicity of a 9000-year-old skeleton are as important to the future of the planet as the radioactive waste from Hanford that has contaminated the region's land and waters. If somehow Native American claims of sovereignty were further eroded, it would open up their lands to new development. Who Kennewick man was is entangled with how and why the sustainability of rivers of the West are endangered.

Black-Indigenous-and-People-of-Color (BIPOC) and White racial identities mutually and negatively reinforce one another, albeit with the power dynamic overwhelmingly favoring the latter category. The Dawes Act allotment policy was coterminous with other policies like the removal of Indian children to boarding schools where they were abused, forbidden from speaking their languages, and severed from their cultural histories and rituals. These coercive practices created a paradoxical system whereby if Indians claimed or were identified as Native American, life on a reservation was one of the few ways to preserve their history and culture. For so many, it was also likely to sentence them to lives of poverty and subsistence. Indian identity was and is also ruthlessly exploited by non-Natives (and some Native Americans) eager to profit from the natural and cultural resources of reservation lands. Blood quantum and tribal enrollment are means to affirm and retain tribal affiliations and to preserve heritage and culture. They are also, as Janet Berlo and Ruth Phillips state, "classic tools of colonial domination." They just as often exclude people "whose ancestry is no more or less mixed than that of those who are legally recognized by laws and policies that derive from outmoded racial theories, patrilineal bias or geographical separation." (Berlo 1998, 19–20) Or, as art critic and curator Paul Chaat Smith insists:

> Authenticity for Indians is a brutal measuring device that says we are only Indian as long as we are authentic. Part of the measurement is about percentage of Indian blood. The more, the better. Fluency in one's Indian language is always a high card. Spiritual practices, living in one's ancestral homeland, attending powwows, all are necessary to ace the authenticity test. Yet many of us believe taking the authenticity test is like drinking the colonizer's Kool-Aid—a practice designed to strengthen our commitment to our own internally warped minds. In this way, we become our own prison guards.
>
> (Smith 2009, 91)

Currently, Pasco and much of Eastern Washington are home to a large and growing number of Hispanic and Latino communities. Franklin County, where Pasco is located, has been a "majority minority" county since 2000, a demographic shift that now characterizes the nation as a whole. Hispanic colonization of the Pacific Northwest predates British, Russian, and French encroachments into the region. Latino families migrated to Eastern Washington throughout the twentieth century, primarily as laborers in the agricultural fields created by redirecting the waters of the Columbia, Snake, Yakima, Walla Walla, and many other rivers. For those who would critique Lin's involvement with the Confluence Project based on her status as an Asian-American woman of Chinese descent, the question of authenticity ultimately misunderstands the artwork's goals. "Confluence" refers not only to those places of contact between different bodies of water but also to the merging of identities and cultures that is the foundation of a shared national identity. The gaps and fissures of American history have been whitewashed by this remarkable fact. Confluence seeks to restore the complexity of the historical record through its installations along the Snake and Columbia Rivers.

References

Berlo, Janet Catherine. 1998. *Native North American Art.* Oxford History of Art, Oxford: Oxford University Press.

Brooks, Joanna. 2004. "Sacajawea, Meet Cogewea: A Red Progressive Revision of Frontier Romance." In *Lewis & Clark: Legacies, Memories, and New Perspectives*, 1st ed. Kris Fresonke and Mark Spence, eds. University of California Press. https://www.jstor.org/stable/10.1525/j.ctt1pnt2f.15

Bulls, Marty Two. 2018. "Kennewick Man and the Long Journey Home." ICT News. September 13, 2018. https://ictnews.org/archive/kennewick-man-and-the-long-journey-home

"Confluence Project Records—Archives West." 2018. WCMss.444-2018-021. Whitman College and Northwest Archives. https://archiveswest.orbiscascade.org/ark:/80444/xv285430

Harden, Blaine. 2012. *A River Lost: The Life and Death of the Columbia.* New York, NY: W.W. Norton & Company.

Hart, Lily, ed. 2022. "Voices of the River Is an Annual Publication by Confluence, a Community-Supported Nonprofit with the Mission to Connect People to the History, Living Cultures, and Ecology of the Columbia River System through Indigenous Voices." 1.

Hunn, Eugene S. 2015. *Čáw Pawá Láakni = They Are Not Forgotten: Sahaptian Place Names Atlas of the Cayuse, Umatilla, and Walla Walla.* Pendleton, OR: Tamástslikt Cultural Institute.

Hyde, Anne Farrar. 2022. *Born of Lakes and Plains: Mixed-Descent Peoples and the Making of the American West.* New York, NY: W.W. Norton & Company, Inc.

Josephy, Alvin M., and Marc Jaffe. 2006. *Lewis and Clark through Indian Eyes.* New York, NY: Knopf.

Kubik, Barbara. 2001. "Sacajawea State Park: '… A Very Pleasant Situated Place.'" Box 8, Folder 35.

"Maya Lin: The Art of Remembrance." 2018. What It Takes®. 2018. Accessed October 19, 2023. https://whatittakes.simplecast.com/episodes/268a00fc

Meyer, Bette Eunice. 1983. *Ainsworth, a Railroad Town.* Fairfield, WA: Ye Galleon Press.

Smith, Paul Chaat. 2009. "Everything You Know about Indians Is Wrong." In *Indigenous Americas.* Minneapolis, MN: University of Minnesota Press.

5   The Listening Circle at Chief Timothy Park

"Not Much to It"?

The boxes, folders, documents, spreadsheets, site plans, and maquettes housed in the Confluence Project archives at Whitman College also include several terabytes (TB) worth of "digital born media" files. Digital-born media is an archival term for materials that originated in digital format. These include video, photographs, slide presentations, emails, and audio recordings. The video content varies from polished promotional documentaries to B-roll footage used for background research or coverage of dedication ceremonies, to name several examples. Digital image files include those made by professional photographers as well as amateur snapshots taken by employees or board members at special events or site visits. In one of these files is a group of satellite images of different locations along the Snake and Columbia Rivers. The images were compiled by Alling Henning Associates, a Northwest media relations firm contracted by the Confluence Project during the early stages of development. The 12 images in the folder include already-chosen and potential locations for Confluence river sites. Pictured are dams, locks, spillways and jetties, agricultural fields and crop circles, runways, warehouses, train tracks, housing developments, and man-made lagoons and harbors. All these facilities are bounded by less developed territory or wildlands, but the targeting of hyper-industrialized spaces provides an indication of what Lin and her team were searching for as they began their work: the extraordinarily ordinary infrastructures that facilitate modern life.

The Listening Circle at Chief Timothy Park was completed in 2015 and is the easternmost Confluence site. The installation is a ten-minute drive from the Clarkston-Lewiston metropolitan area that straddles the Washington-Idaho border, taking their name from the eponymous explorers. It is located on Silcott Island, an islet overlooking the Snake River near the confluence of the Clearwater River. Lewiston bills itself as "Idaho's Only Seaport," linking the cities via the Snake and Columbia Rivers to the Pacific Ocean. The Listening Circle is a large outdoor amphitheater with curved basalt benches etched with quotes from Clark's description of the nearby locations, taxonomies of

DOI: 10.4324/9781003309024-6

plants and animals, topographical information, and a record of encounters between the Corps of Discovery and the local Native tribes. Unlike most amphitheaters, the layout is not oriented unidirectionally toward a stage. Instead, three rows of basalt benches face each other in a stepped pattern that seems to move outward from the center like ripples in a pond. The base of the benches in the first rows are flush with the ground. The second set of stepped rows is approximately ten feet behind the first and extends longer at either side, sloping upward at a slight five-degree grade. The pattern of longer stepped benches is repeated for the third rows. The effect is very subtle, so much so that a park manager was recently quoted in a local newspaper: "The park is nice, but as far as the circle, I don't know what you'd drive out here to look at, frankly. There's not much to it." (Tribune 2017)

If a visit to Sacajawea State Park is to be engulfed in the sights, sounds, and smells of the Columbia River's anthropogenic signifiers, by contrast, Chief Timothy Park is characterized by its comparatively serene setting. Confluence promotional materials describe this location as "most closely resembling the landscape seen by Lewis and Clark." As this book argues, Lin's installations are built to blend in with their surroundings, including the human-made infrastructures that now form an iconography of industrialization characteristic of the contemporary river systems of the Columbia and Snake. They do not attempt to mask this mechanical mise-en-scene. They eschew the spectacle of much contemporary artwork, which tends frequently to dominate our field of vision at the expense of the surrounding context. (Monuments and memorials are particular examples of this phenomenon, with the Vietnam Veteran's Memorial being a rare exception that proves the rule.) While this iconography may be less apparent at Chief Timothy, it is nonetheless ever-present in myriad other ways.

The serene waterline and slow current are products of the four dams along the Lower Snake River in Washington State. These dams provide hydropower and electricity for much of the tri-state region of Eastern Washington, Oregon, and Idaho, turning many stretches of river into "lakes" suitable for boating, barges, and recreation. They have also been the primary agent threatening salmon and other species vital to the ecological health of the region. Over the past decade, plans have been drafted for the removal of the Lower Snake dams; however, a new industrial use that requires regulated, stable waterflows has quickly become a potential hurdle. In December 2016, Meta (the parent company of Facebook) announced it would build a new industrial park and data center in Kuna, Idaho, near the Snake River. Data centers, or server farms as they are also known, make up the virtual linked network storage spaces known as "The Cloud." Meta's data center, and others like it owned by Microsoft, Amazon, and Apple are "where the cloud lives," to quote a recent tech blog. They are "the physical manifestation of the Internet, often located in rural areas offering cheap land and power." (Dommann, Rickli, and Stadler 2020) Perhaps the most important requirement of these data centers is the constant, unquenchable supply of water needed to cool the tens of thousands of motors that power individual servers, keeping the Cloud aloft in our minds but also forever tied to material conditions along the river. These hulking, steel-reinforced concrete bunkers are rapidly becoming part of the iconography of the Northwest, and other rural regions adjacent to major river systems throughout the United States.

This chapter will analyze the Confluence installation at Chief Timothy Park, the most rural of all the extant built artworks. It will provide a history of the Nez Perce who have lived here for millennia, whose lives were, and are, inextricably tied to the lands of the Columbia River Plateau, and who continue to fight for the sustainability of the rivers that bind their lands. The Listening Circle's design is rooted in the rituals and songs of the Nez Perce. As such, this chapter will depart slightly from previous ones through a discussion of the dedication ceremonies held at this location and their importance to understanding and interpreting the artwork. Lewis and Clark's perilous passage over the Bitterroot Mountains, down the Lolo Trail, into lands inhabited by Nez Perce and affiliated tribes, signaled a pivotal historical event for these peoples. But as many scholars note, their lives had already been transformed by centuries of colonial contact that brought horses, disease, metals, religion, and weapons. This chapter will explain how the Corps of Discovery carried in their wake over a century of hardship and tragedy which the Nez Perce spent the last several decades attempting to move beyond. The sparsely populated lands of what would become Idaho, Washington, and Oregon were misperceived as a tabula rasa on which to inscribe modernity's progress. Finally, the chapter will conclude with a discussion of the different types of industrialization, including data centers and Cloud infrastructure. It is, ironically, this very same infrastructure that houses the data files archived at Whitman College, which I wrote about above, and that risks perpetuating the inertia of indifference that characterizes this moment of crisis.

From Skybowl to Listening Circle: Maya Lin at Chief Timothy Park

A Confluence Project newsletter sent in 2005 describes the amphitheater to be built at Chief Timothy Park as a "skybowl" designed to "tell the history of the Nez Perce people." Two years later, fundraising solicitations and press releases were calling it a "listening circle." ("Confluence Project Records—Archives West" n.d., Box 7, Folder 10) The reasons for this change are unclear, although it does coincide with a rhetorical shift toward listening and hearing that appears more frequently in the archival materials. Sound plays an important role at every Confluence location as previous chapters have attested. The early design plans for Chief Timothy refer to the shape of the amphitheater from an overhead position as resembling sound waves. The site

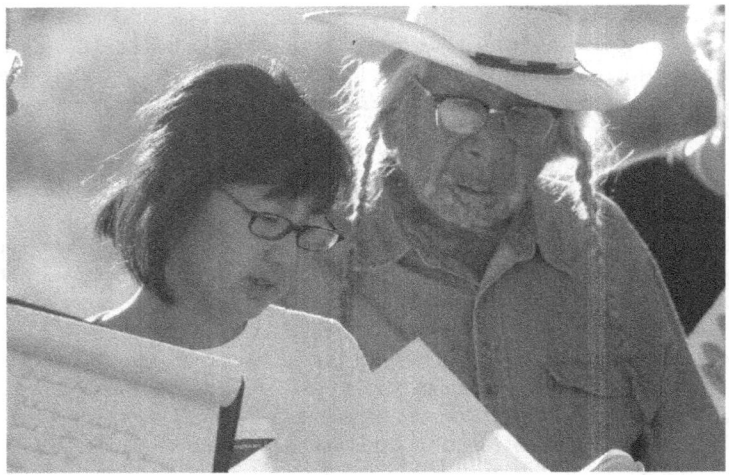

Figure 5.1 Maya Lin and Horace P. Axtell (Nez Perce) visiting the future site of the Listening Circle at Chief Timothy Park, ca. 2005.

Sources: Photographer unknown. Confluence Digital 2018-021-31, WCMss444. Confluence Project Records.

Whitman College and Northwest Archives.

was developed in consultation with tribal elders of the Nez Perce, in particular Horace Axtell, who also led a blessing ceremony at the location Figure 5.1. Both Lin and Axtell expressed hope that the Listening Circle would inspire dialogue and reflection about the region's Indigenous cultures. "Maybe we'll be able to tell the story of our people," Axtell has said. "And people will understand that we were the ones who were here before—when our language was the only one heard in the canyons." (Raymond 2007) Since its completion, the amphitheater has been used for gatherings featuring songs, storytelling, meetings, and concerts.

If the visual is somehow precluded at the Listening Circle, how are we meant to experience the artwork there and what is it we should be listening for? To address these questions, it is important to attend to the work itself, but not just the work, the experience of the park and its surroundings as well. To get to Chief Timothy Park from the highway, visitors must cross a short bridge and enter past a kiosk to parking lots at the base of a half-mile trailhead leading to the artwork. (Chief Timothy Park is the only Confluence site not owned by Oregon or Washington. The land is owned and leased by the Army Corps of Engineers to a camping and recreational company who manage its facilities.) An alternative lot on the opposite side provides access for disabled visitors. The trail runs alongside the Snake with spectacular views of the river, the surrounding canyons and the steep, tree-less mountains. Here, Lin worked with a local landscaping company, Greenworks LLC, to restore Native grass and shrub and to revitalize camas, a crucial food source for all Plateau tribes. An osprey nest that predates Confluence sits atop a reinforced poll at the trail's crest. The birds are regular companions during walks to the site, flying out over the edge or looking down from a perch composed of the detritus of campers and boaters: colorful, frayed ropes and ties are woven into the nest's architecture of sticks and twigs. Grass and shrub-covered hills shelter the island on all but the eastern side. Distant noise from the highway across the river, a few standalone homes on the nearby hillsides, an occasional fishing boat or barge are among the few visible or audible indicators of modernity's encroachment.

The trail is designed for a specific entry-point to the amphitheater, although there are no fences or markers to dictate the approach. The path is inspired by traditional Nez Perce tribal ceremonies in which elders faced west in a place of authority and respect, women faced north, and men faced south. The east side was left open as a welcome to the sunrise and new day. No one was permitted to enter the ceremony by passing behind those already in attendance. The pathway descends gradually toward the edge of the amphitheater and the basalt benches. Text is carved along the interior side of the stone facing the ring's center. The innermost north-facing half-ring states, "The Nez Perce blessed this site for the Confluence Project on April 30, 2005. This earthwork commemorates the ceremony…" Directly opposite, the inner south-facing ring features a quote from Lewis's journal dated May 4, 1806: "… the hills of the creek which we descended this morning are high and in most parts rocky and abrupt." The middle half-ring provides a passage from Clark's journal entry about the Corps' first view of the location from two miles upstream: "worthy of remark that not one stick of timber on the river near the forks and but a fiew trees for a great distance up the River." (Lewis, et al., May 4, 1806 entry in The Journals of the Lewis and Clark Expedition 2005)

The diameter of the amphitheater is over a 100 feet from the longest point of the outer rings. As with every site, reading the entire text requires walking the circles, stooping or bending to take in the words, moving back and forth along the different levels, and taking in the surroundings. This process is reinforced by the quotations that ask viewers to imagine what the Corps of Discovery members saw, how they interacted with the land and Nez Perce peoples, and how the surroundings are remarkably similar to what they were two centuries ago. And like the other sites, this experience can be profound for those attuned to or open to a different interaction with art, space, and place. Of all the Confluence sites, the Listening Circle is the most likely to be overlooked. This soft footprint is wholly intended, despite criticisms that there is little to see. If, from Cape Disappointment to Chief Timothy, the Confluence Project can be characterized as a progression of art installations with a staged decrease in infrastructural impacts at each location as one proceeds east from Cape Disappointment, then the Listening Circle is a logical culmination of this sequence.

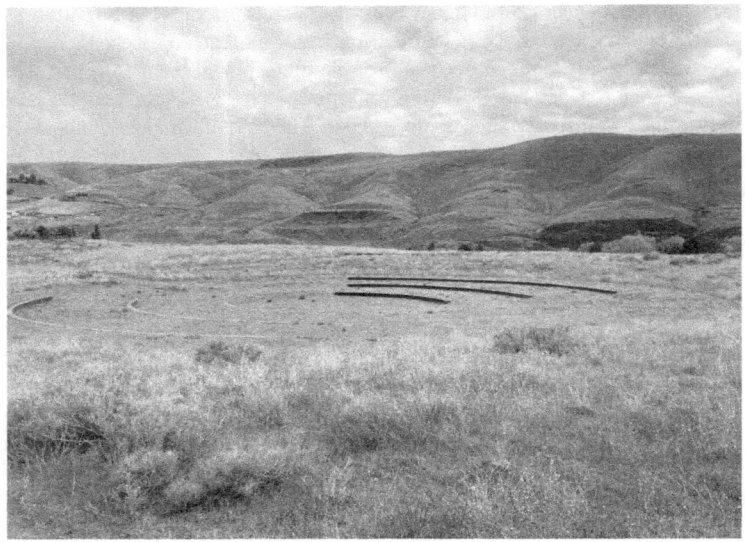

Figure 5.2 The Listening Circle, May 2023.
Sources: Photo by author.

That the Listening Circle is also defined as an amphitheater foregrounds its value as a space of performance Figure 5.2. The importance of the blessing ceremony is emphasized by its inclusion as carved text on the benches. This ceremony and the Listening Circle's dedication a decade later provide a frame for better understanding of the role of sound, hearing, listening, and the sharing of stories at the site. The blessing ceremony in 2005 included many Nez Perce constituents as well as city and state officials from the surrounding region. Guests of honor included Wilfred Scott, Executive Committee member of the Nez Perce tribe and a project liaison, Axtel, and numerous other tribal elders and councilmembers. A Native drum circle was accompanied by songs and chants. Indigenous scholars Alan Marshall and Samuel Watters write of the importance of song to the Nez Perce: "Families shared songs that were unique to their histories; power songs, historical songs, and spirit and dance songs that also related Nimiipuu histories. There were drumming songs, medicine or healing songs, holy songs, songs that honored the elements, and courting songs. Songs that honored all life, told of the past, and told of all of the earth's creatures, and recorded histories." (Willard, Marshall, and Pearson 2020, 40) Historian Alvin Josephy, Jr. explains the inextricable connections between song, dance, and place for Nez Perce identity: "Growing up I often heard wind through the river maples combine with Nez Perce traditional songs, but it wasn't until I heard them sung along the Clearwater or Snake rivers that I realized that the drumming and singing were shaped by these particular places." Language, too, was the "voice of the land and its creatures," he adds, formed by generations of "listening to the world around them …" (Josephy and Jaffe 2006, x) Sound scholar Dylan Robinson states that Indigenous song also conveys laws, medicine, and myths and, in some cases, serves as primary historical documentation. (Robinson 2020, 8)

Blessings occurred at all the Confluence locations, including Celilo Park. Dedication ceremonies were also held at all the extant sites. Ceremonial activities are common for large projects of all kinds, but the characters of the Confluence blessings and dedications are unique in their acknowledgment of Indigenous land and customs that predate American colonial expansion. On the day I attended the 2015 dedication, approximately 150 people gathered to hear brief talks by local tribal leaders Antone Minthorn, Anthony Johnson (Chairman of the Nez Perce Executive Committee), Wilfred Scott, Confluence Project Director Colin Fogarty, a Lewis and Clark historical re-enactor, and Lin herself. The Waahp Qahqun Drum group's performance bookended the ceremony with the sounds of singing and chanting. Their songs were both celebratory and mournful, giving the proceedings a somber, meditative tone. For example, when the color guard presented the flags (including those of both the nations of the Nez Perce and the United States), instead of the national anthem, a song that commemorated the Stevens Treaty of 1855 that resulted in displacement and containment of the tribes within reservation lands was performed. The juxtaposition between the solemn singing and chanting and the formal patriotism of the flag bearers, themselves Nez Perce members and Vietnam War veterans, created a dissonant moment, recalling Daehnke's similar critique of the dedication of the Land Bridge in Chapter 2.

Oral traditions, including songs and music, are central to Native American cultures. Colonization of Indian lands, violent displacement and removal to reservations (often in unfamiliar geographic regions), and Bureau of Indian Affairs policies that sought to sever Indians from their own languages and customs disrupted nearly every aspect of daily life for all Native Americans, including the Nez Perce. That these ceremonies took place on land owned by the federal government might signify incremental improvements between sovereign Native American nations and communities and the agencies that oversaw some of the worst transgressions of treaty rights over the past century-and-a-half, however marginal or ceremonial such meetings may seem. Ideally, the Listening Circle is built for just such opportunities, creating space for new dialogues and exchanges between sovereign Indian nations and communities and the descendants of settler colonists.

Public Art as Dialogue

Dialogue and reflection are partners to listening. As such, Confluence evokes a subgenre of public art that strives for a more inclusive, collaborative, and reciprocal practice.

The ceremonies and performances at Chief Timothy Park have value beyond the physical properties of the artwork itself. The Circle provides a means for reclaiming Nez Perce traditions, a sacred space for reconnecting to the past, reflecting on the present, and planning for the future. There is also a sonic register beyond the experience of live performance, as sound art historian Lutz Koepnick writes about the site: "… the sounds Lin's Listening Circle wants us to attend to aren't just exterior sounds or cochlear transmissions, but inaudible echoes of the past and imperceptible resonances in the present— a soundscape that exceeds the ears …" (Koepnick 2022) He describes this as a "silence" that still reverberates, still resonates, while acknowledging that non-Native listeners are unlikely to hear or sense these echoes. Koepnick uses the term silence, but the songs and chants of the Nez Perce are not silent and serve as opportunities to rebuild and attend to the two centuries of transformation brought about by settler colonialism.

Scholars like Miwon Kwon and Grant Kester write that debates about site-specific work in the 1970s and 1980s made way for "New Genre Public Art," a variation characterized by its "foregrounding [of] social issues and political activism, and/or for engaging 'community' collaborations." (Kwon 2002) One of New Genre's most vital features was its inclusiveness: women and artists of color found new ways to produce and exhibit work outside of more conservative artworld institutions. As such, they were also able to address pressing social problems, often around race and gender. Suzanne Lacy, a practitioner of the New Genre mode who popularized the term, produced works that confronted specific social issues and were defined by their pedagogical, collaborative, and limited life span. Three Weeks in May (1977) was a multimedia piece that used performance, graffiti, maps, and other staged events for local newspapers and television stations that otherwise ignored the alarming frequency of rape and sexual assault in Los Angeles. The Oakland Projects (1991–2001) brought together Oakland youth, civic leaders, activists, residents, and members of the Oakland Police Department over the course of a decade to collaborate on a series of conversations, performances, videos, workshops, and other forms of "interventions." The goal was to address educational opportunity, gang violence, police brutality, mutual mistrust, and shared antipathies among the participants. Kester advanced Lacy's theories about New Genre by calling this kind of practice "diaological" or "conversational." He defines dialogical work as one that "unfolds through a process of performative interaction" via "dialogue and collaboration." For him, the value of the work lies in its emphasis "on the character of the interaction, not the physical or formal integrity of a given artifact or the artist's experience in producing it." ("Conversation Piecesducing inity and Communication in Modern Art—Whitman College" 2004, 10) While The Oakland Projects did produce work that was displayed in galleries and can now be viewed on Lacy's own Vimeo channel, the collaborative, performative nature of the project sought to downplay the reification of the object and the authorial hierarchies of the museum and gallery world. (Lacy 2023)

The Chief Timothy installation draws on the traditions of site-specific, New Genre, and the Dialogical in its foregrounding of listening as a central activity of conversation and understanding. Where Confluence differs from much of Lin's previous work is in its dialogical dimensions. In the two decades since the initial groundbreaking, the Confluence Project has also emphasized educational outreach, cultural programming at the national park sites and affiliated institutions, trail and site maintenance volunteer opportunities, lectures, story gatherings, plant walks, and first food events, to name only a few recent efforts. In effect, the earthworks have become totems around which these activities take place. In addition to the dedication ceremony, the site has hosted other performances as well. In September 2017, pianist Hunter Noack performed classical and contemporary compositions at the Listening Circle. The music was simultaneously livestreamed to headphones, so visitors might also wander the landscape during the performance. Led by Executive Director Colin Fogarty and Program Manager Courtney Yilk, this large-scale, ongoing community outreach programming maintains a focus on the issues at the core of the Confluence Project during long periods between construction and installation of the actual earthworks themselves. At a lecture given at the Seattle Art Museum in 2015, Lin noted that her goal was to "disappear" from these locations, which I take to mean an effort to downplay her authorial presence in favor of the historicization of the sites that occurs in the didactic text found at each location. (Lin 2015)

The Nez Perce before and after Lewis and Clark

"Nez Perce" is a label given to a group of affiliated Native American bands of the Columbia River Plateau by French trappers prior to contact by the Corps of Discovery expedition. It is a term of misrecognition and misapplication that refers to the body modification practice of "pierced noses" characteristic of some Chinook tribes along the Pacific coast. Instead, "Niimíipuu" is a more accurate term frequently translated as "the people" and refers to a group of loosely affiliated Sahaptin-speaking bands whose territory encompassed vast swaths of land in present-day Idaho, Montana, southeastern Washington, and northeastern Oregon. (There are multiple spellings of Niimíipuu. I am using the label Nez Perce for consistency's sake in relation to the language used by the Confluence Project.) The Nez Perce were connected through intermarriage, shared customs, and lifeways with many other regional bands, including the Coeur d'Alenes, Spokans, Flatheads, Wallawallas, Palouses, Umatillas, Yakamas, and Cayuses. (Josephy and Jaffe 2006, 2)

Those tribal lifeways include a spirituality rooted in animism, a deep connection to the waters and rivers of the Columbia Plateau, and a common identity interwoven with the region's topography. Josephy, Jr. states that, like most Native American cultures, the Nez Perce believe that every living and nonliving thing in the sky and on the land possesses a spirit. Not only humans but also animals, fish, trees, rocks, rivers, lakes, and stars are unique agentic entities interconnected within a larger cosmological system. (Josephy and Jaffe 2006, 17) Historians Allen Pinkham and Steven Evans describe the Nez Perce relation to streams and rivers as "the threads that held life together...a powerful and mysterious force that bound the sky to the earth." (Pinkham 2013, 84) The Clearwater, Lower Snake, and mid-Columbia rivers were unique territories as well as part of the overall lifeblood of the Plateau. Tribes understood the seasonal properties of each ecology and were attuned to the vast changes that took place in these environments over the course of time. (Pinkham 2013, 38) Historian J. Diane Pearson said that this holistic worldview tied the Nez Perce to their surroundings, insisting that they understand human beings as "part of, rather than an imposition on, their environments." (Willard et al. 2020, 33)

The introduction of the horse to North America sometime around 1700 vastly transformed the region's tribes. The Nez Perce, Cayuse, and Umatilla bands in particular became wealthy, powerful communities as a result of their skillful incorporation of horses into their cultures. The role of horses in the Corps of Discovery expedition is often ignored, but the animals were vital to the success of their mission. They were used for mapping surveys and to track and hunt game. They carried provisions and helped pull canoes and boats through treacherous currents. And, occasionally in desperate situations, horses were killed and eaten to sustain the expedition's crew. When Lewis and Clark reached Nez Perce territory, they were awed by the tribe's prowess with the animals and recognized the wealth and prestige they were afforded as a result. After Indians informed the Corps of Discovery that travel on the Snake and Columbia Rivers would not be practicable for horses, enough trust had been built up between them and the Nez Perce that Lewis and Clark felt confident in leaving their herd under the tribe's care over the winter of 1805–06.

Pinkham and Evans write that "the case can be made that [Lewis and Clark's] time with the Nez Perce was both the most important and the most satisfying of the transcontinental journey." (Pinkham 2013, xiii) They calculate that the Corps spent more time with the tribe than any other Indigenous peoples during their journey, nourishing them back to health after the perilous trip over the Bitteroots and Lolo Trail, sharing their vast knowledge of the region with the crew members, and helping them build canoes for river travel. [xiii, 33] This time was not without tensions, however. A number of Nez Perce proposed killing the crew until a tribal elder who had lived among settlers in Eastern territories intervened. Pinkham also describes "the puppy incident" in which an enraged Lewis was confronted by a young tribal member for killing and eating a young girl's pet. (Pinkham 2013, 153) Nez Perce oral traditions also assert that Clark fathered a child by the daughter of Red Bear, a chief and leader, during his time with the tribe. The boy's name was Halatookit ("Daytime Smoker"). (Josephy and Jaffe 2006, 159) His patrilineal heritage was never officially recorded in settler territorial documents.

Present when Lewis and Clark arrived at Alpowai Village was the young son of Chief Ta-Moots-Tsoo, known by the same name. He would take the name of Chief Timothy as an adult after converting to Christianity some 30 years after the Corps made their way through the region. Chief Timothy is known to be the first Nez Perce member to convert at the urgings of Presbyterian missionary Henry Spalding, a fact that makes him a controversial figure, an appeaser, but also may explain why an island near Clarkston is named in his honor. He never achieved the same renown as his tribal kin Chief Joseph and Smohalla, who agitated and fought against relocation and settler colonial encroachments. Like them, however, Chief Timothy's lifespan overlapped the nineteenth century's treaty era, a shameful period in the nation's history during which agreements between tribal nations and the federal government were brokered, their terms ignored or disregarded (always to the benefit of settlers), and wars waged as a result of broken promises. The discovery of gold on Indian land in Orofino territory abrogated the Nez Perce Treaty of 1855, reducing the size of the Nez Perce reservation and allowing miners to travel and claim lands pledged to the tribe.

In 1862, President Lincoln signed the Homestead Act into law, encouraging settler migration and land ownership for American citizens in the West, excluding Indians who were not designated citizens. By 1871, the federal government abolished the treaty process altogether, allowing "agreements" by Executive Order pertaining to the creation or redefinition of reservations. Reservation lands were established, then reestablished as soon as (White) settlers found value not previously recognized. Many of these orders made provisions for expanding the railroads to more easily connect the rich natural resources of the West with the industrial centers of the East. Finally, in 1887, the Dawes Act opened up reservation lands to non-Indian ownership that was ostensibly a means of pillaging the meager resources left to Native Americans in the Northwest territories, all of which set the stage for the rapid industrial growth of the Columbia Plateau that would take place throughout the twentieth century.

"Where the Cloud Lives": Industrial Transformations of the Columbia Plateau

From its inception to the present, the Confluence Project centers the "Columbia River system" as the site of Lin's earthworks and the organization's ongoing activities. The Snake River has largely been the focus of this chapter. It may seem odd for readers unfamiliar with the Pacific Northwest to understand both the connections and the distinctions between the two. The Snake River is the Columbia's largest tributary and, as such, shares many of the features that characterize the larger river system. These include flora and fauna, mineralogical deposits, and, for at least the last 10,000 years, the peoples and cultures who inhabit the Columbia Plateau region. The Plateau refers to the geologic and geographic territory formed millions of years ago by basaltic lava floods from the late Miocene and early Pliocene volcanic eruptions. The Columbia River runs south from the Canadian Rockies before veering west, where it cuts through the Cascades mountain range on its way to the Pacific. While I do not wish to elide the differences between the two rivers, their surroundings, or inhabitants, this analysis will focus instead on the interconnections between the two environments, what Harden calls the "Columbia-Snake River system" (Harden 2012, 52), and the industrial development responsible for the comorbidity factors that contribute to the climate crisis.

Previous chapters have addressed how dams transformed the Plateau region and beyond, as is the case with the global repercussions of plutonium refinement and nuclear power generated at Hanford. The Columbia River System's 14 dams reinvented the high desert terrain as a fertile agricultural zone. The cheap hydropower generated by these dams played an enormous role in growing the economies of the entire Northwest. Relative to nuclear and coal-fired power plants, dams produce considerably less greenhouse gasses. The sheer size and scale of the Grand Coulee Dam, the Columbia's largest, provided steady employment during the Great Depression, achieving fame as the subject of folk singer Woody Guthrie's series of songs about its construction, including "Roll On, Columbia, Roll On." It is still one of the largest dams in the world in terms of the generating capacity of its three power stations. There are 60 dams throughout the Columbia River watershed, which include the Snake, Salmon, Owyhee, and Boise rivers with the Columbia and Snake accounting for 31 of the 60.

The Center for Land Use Interpretation (CLUI) is an organization devoted to interpreting the built environment's visual landscapes. It produces images, exhibitions, books, and tours that perform an infrastructural hermeneutics. CLUI deliberately positions itself in a gray zone between an arts organization and a quasi-public agency. Founder and director Matthew Coolidge describes CLUI's mission in terms similar to Lin's attempts to understand landscape through the lens of technology and human development. "Repeated travel over the same road increases our familiarity with it, and we think we come to know it better and better. But patterns and ways of seeing can form, regulating our perceptive apparatus in ways that limit our ability to sense the rest of the spectrum." (Coolidge and Simons 2006, 31) CLUI trains its gaze on those sites and locations that most people are conditioned to ignore or avoid but that nevertheless shape our daily lives in profound ways, i.e., refineries, military bases, corporate headquarters, shipyards, landfills, nuclear power plants, toxic waste facilities, data centers, dams, as well as structures usually categorized as "art."

In 1999, CLUI published *100 Places in Washington*, a book containing photographs and concise, pithy descriptions of their function. It resembles a Baedeker's for the post-apocalypse or a Lonely Planet Guide to the Anthropocene. Each entry features one representative photo sourced from Creative Commons and the accompanying descriptions are usually no more than a few sentences. The cumulative effect of juxtaposing a place like Goldendale Aluminum Plant Site near John Day Dam alongside Robert Morris's untitled earthwork at Johnson Gravel Pit Number 30 overlooking the Seattle-Tacoma International Airport forces viewers to confront the stereotypes we share between the use value of art—i.e., what does it *do*?—vs. the aesthetic value of monumental infrastructure.

The book features entries for many of the dams of the Columbia Plateau, including Grand Coulee, McNary, and Chief Joseph. The entry for Chief Joseph explains the structure's absence of a fish ladder, noting that it prevents salmon from migrating beyond this point to their natural spawning points further upriver.

The infrastructure documented by CLUI provides critical benefits, but it also comes with extreme costs. A report produced by nature conservation groups Save Our Wild Salmon and Defenders of Wildlife, who advocate for removal of the Lower Snake River dams, states that the Endangered Species Act lists 13 stocks of steelhead and wild salmon as either threatened or endangered, and that the ongoing attempts to restore salmon populations above these dams, where they once thrived, have failed. (Herrman et al. 2022) Harden and historian Richard White have cataloged the efforts—some profound, others absurd—to maintain fish viability in their natural habitats. Both writers chronicle the relationship between the dams and their catastrophic impact on the numerous riverine species, most especially salmon. As recently as the 1990s, so few salmon survived to reach their spawning grounds above the dams that they were treated as anomalies, named, and anthropomorphized in the media. "Sally the Sockeye" and "Lonesome Larry" were the only two wild salmon to reach Redfish Lake in Idaho in 1991 and 1992, respectively. Larry's ignominious end came at the hands of then-Idaho governor Cecil Andrus, who mounted and displayed the fish as a cautionary tale about the dams' effect on the once-abundant salmon populations. (Harden 2012, 31) White describes the smolts and hatcheries that keep salmon populations alive, as well as the actions government agencies take to facilitate their migration. These methods include capturing and carrying them past the concrete barriers via truck or barge to then be re-released downstream beyond the Snake River dams. In other cases, salmon are propelled through plastic flex tubes over spillways and channels that otherwise obstruct their passage. White asserts: "At every phase of their life, they are subject to human intervention and oversight. They are less a wild species than a swimming genetic bank." (White 1996, 105)

Salmon's sustainability requires removal of the dams that prevent their large-scale migration and spawning. The Rube Goldberg-like contraptions that currently provide assistance to migrating fish cannot achieve the results to scale required to maintain thriving fish populations. Recently, bipartisan political efforts between Democratic and Republican state officials in Idaho and Washington, the Nez Perce, and the U.S. Army Corps of Engineers have made progress in plans to remove the Lower Snake River Dams. Removal of the Lower Monumental, Little Goose, Ice Harbor, and Lower Granite Dams would restore 144 miles of free-flowing water and allow more than 14,000 acres of inundated lands to re-emerge, including the Nez Perce village of Alpowai where Chief Timothy's band lived until shortly after his death in 1891. The Nez Perce are leading the way in dam removal efforts, in part through Project 5311 which seeks to replace the 5311 Megawatts of hydropower with solar and battery storage facilities. At the time of this writing, Project 5311 intends to employ Native Americans, and 10 percent of the electricity will be reserved for the Nez Perce reservation.

How to Listen to a Cloud? How to Hear a Salmon? How to Remove a Dam?

The awkwardly named Inflation Reduction Act, signed into law by President Joe Biden in 2022, will provide massive federal funding for renewable energy projects across the country. The bill will subsidize urgently needed expansions to solar and wind facilities in an attempt to wean us off of our collective reliance on fossil fuels. Replacing hydropower with solar creates many opportunities to reimagine the human-built infrastructures contributing to species decline and the climate crisis. However, the removal of dams is now complicated by a new dependency on digital computing's expanding infrastructure. The data storage facilities that house internet servers and support network connectivity are appearing with ever-greater frequency along the Snake and Columbia Rivers, and other water systems across the United States. Literature and media theorist Tung-Hui Hu argues that the "legacy of the cloud has already begun to write itself into the real environment." In addition to their reliance on already stressed water systems in the West and elsewhere, data centers accounted for 2 percent of global greenhouse gas emissions in 2008, "and data centers have grown exponentially since then." (Hu 2015, xxv) More recent research has found that computational resources needed to train large-scale Artificial Intelligence (AI) models doubled every 3.4 years since 2012. (Hao 2019) AI's rapid expansion in 2023, along with storage-dependent technologies like cryptocurrencies and video conferencing—made essential during the COVID-19 pandemic—are putting even greater pressure on technology companies to grow this infrastructure. Alphabet, Google's parent corporation, was recently forced to disclose that its enormous server farm in The Dalles, Oregon, uses nearly 25 percent of the town's water supply. The building site also sits atop the inundated rock formations and channels that made up the rapids of Celilo Falls. Such contradictions are symptomatic of the collective entanglements that contribute to climate change and make us all complicit to some degree in the ongoing crisis.

If, as the park manager quoted at the beginning of this chapter, it is correct that there is not much to look at when visiting the Chief Timothy installation, then maybe we are looking at the wrong things. Or maybe we should be attentive to how the Listening Circle reminds us that looking is only part of how we make sense of ourselves and our environment. Sound art uses the terms critical listening, deep listening, and active listening to describe a practice of defamiliarizing oneself from the sonic emissions of our everyday lives so that we can pay closer attention to environmental factors that may often go unheard or unnoticed. Composer Pauline Oliveros developed a practice of deep listening that began from earlier experiments she conducted and recorded in her book Sonic Meditations. Like John Cage, Oliveros was influenced by Asian philosophies, in particular the contemplative practices associated with Buddhism. Published in 1971, *Sonic Meditations* contained "verbal descriptions of how to listen and create sound fabrics in groups" using improvisational, inclusive methods. (Brunner 2006, 716) In the late 1980s, she developed her theories of Deep Listening based in part on these earlier experiments and published them in *Deep Listening: A Composer's Sound Practice.* She defines the activity of Deep Listening as "having to do with complexity and boundaries, or edges beyond ordinary or habitual understandings." She goes on to say it is "learning to expand the perception of sounds to include the whole space/time continuum of sound." (Oliveros 2005, xxiii)

Oliveros's book contains a number of prompts, reminiscent of Fluxus event scores, that call on participants to combine breathing, bodily movement, and techniques to focus attention to create heightened awareness of one's environment. In *Earth: Sensing/Listening/Sounding*, she instructs participants to lie in a circle on their backs with their heads facing the center of the room.

> Can you imagine listening to all that is sounding as if your body were the whole earth? There might be the sounds of your own thoughts or of your body, natural sounds of birds and animals, voices, sounds of electrical appliances and machines. Some sounds might be very faint, some very intense, some continuous, and some intermittent. As you are listening globally, can you imagine that you can use any sound that you hear as a cue either to relax your body more deeply or to energize it?
>
> (Oliveros 2005, 32)

Oliveros implies here that listening is a call to act, either to relax or become energized, so that one is prepared to take part in a larger social or communal activity. The Listening Circle, like all of the Confluence sites, asks us to listen to those Plateau tribal communities and lifeways who existed on these rivers and lands sustainably for thousands of years. The work encourages a matter-of-fact, unromantic perspective about how we got in the mess we're in, while also calling us to action to ensure that we don't make it any worse than it already is. The activism of Lin's sound work is urging us to hear, to hear what we can't hear, and then to work to change the trajectory of decline and crisis.

References

Brunner, Lance. 2006. "Deep Listening: A Composer's Sound Practice." *Music Library Association. Notes* 62 (3): 715–18. https://doi.org/10.1353/not.2006.0007

"Confluence Project Records—Archives West." 2018. WCMss.444-2018-021. Whitman College and Northwest Archives. https://archiveswest.orbiscascade.org/ark:/80444/xv285430

Coolidge, Matthew, and Sarah Simons. 2006. *Overlook: Exploring the Internal Fringes of America with the Center for Land Use Interpretation*. New York, NY: Metropolis Books.

Dommann, Monika, Hannes Rickli, and Max Stadler. 2020. *Data Centers: Edges of a Wired Nation*. Zurich: Lars Müller Publishers.

Hao, Karen. 2019. The Computing Power Needed to Train AI Is Now Rising Seven Times Faster than Ever Before. MIT Technology Review. Accessed May 4, 2022. https://www.technologyreview.com/2019/11/11/132004/the-computing-power-needed-to-train-ai-is-now-rising-seven-times-faster-than-ever-before/

Harden, Blaine. 2012. *A River Lost: The Life and Death of the Columbia*. New York, NY: W.W. Norton & Company.

Herrman, Carrie, Robb Krehbiel, Mae Lacey, Sam Mace, and Lindsay Rosa. 2022. "Imagining a New Future for the Lower Snake River."

Hu, Tung-Hui. 2015. *A Prehistory of the Cloud*. Cambridge, MA: The MIT Press.

Josephy, Alvin M., and Marc Jaffe. 2006. *Lewis and Clark through Indian Eyes*. New York, NY: Knopf.

Kester, Grant. 2004. "Conversation Pieces: Community and Communication in Modern Art—Whitman College." 2004. https://sherlock.whitman.edu/permalink/01ALLIANCE_WHITC/1aivab7/alma9929528701867

Koepnick, Lutz. 2022. "Listening to Silence at the Confluence Project." All Around Sound. Accessed November 25, 2022. https://www.allaroundsound-bloomsbury.com/2022/11/25/listening-to-the-confluence-project-part-1-by-lutz-koepnick/

Kwon, Miwon. 2002. *One Place after Another: Site-Specific Art and Locational Identity*. Cambridge, MA: MIT Press.

Lin, Maya. 2015. "Public Talk: Seattle Art Museum." Seattle Art Museum, July 29.

"May 4, 1806 | Journals of the Lewis and Clark Expedition." n.d. Accessed October 18, 2023. https://lewisandclarkjournals.unl.edu/item/lc.jrn.1806-05-04

Oliveros, Pauline. 2005. *Deep Listening: A Composer's Sound Practice*. Bloomington, IN: iUniverse, Inc.

Pinkham, Allen. 2013. "Lewis and Clark among the Nez Perce: Strangers in the Land of the Nimiipuu." In *Ron Laycock Collection of Lewis and Clark Literature*. Washburn, ND: The Dakota Institute Press of the Lewis & Clark Fort Mandan Foundation.

Productions, Leaf Street, dir. 2023. *Suzanne Lacy—The Oakland Projects—Gallery Video*. Accessed March 22, 2019. https://vimeo.com/799537677

Raymond, Camila. 2007. The Shape of Memory. Portland Monthly. Accessed March 16, 2021. https://www.pdxmonthly.com/arts-and-culture/2009/05/1107-features-memory

Robinson, Dylan. 2020. "Hungry Listening: Resonant Theory for Indigenous Sound Studies." In *Indigenous Americas*. Minneapolis, MN: University of Minnesota Press.

Tribune, KERRI SANDAINE of the. 2017. "Park Works to Draw Attention to 'Listening Circle.'" The Lewiston Tribune. Accessed April 10, 2017. https://www.lmtribune.com/northwest/park-works-to-draw-attention-to-listening-circle/article_e6c000e3-2efd-5008-beb7-45dbd02d8d22.html

White, Richard. 1996. *The Organic Machine*. A Critical Issue. New York, NY: Hill and Wang.

Willard, William, Alan G. Marshall, and J. Diane Pearson. 2020. *Rising from the Ashes: Survival, Sovereignty, and Native America*. Lincoln, NC: University of Nebraska Press.

6 Reflections on Confluence's Material and Immaterial Value

Unbuilt Confluence

From the outset, Lin and her collaborative team envisioned seven physical locations for the Confluence Project. This would include the installation at Celilo Falls and an environmental research center at Frenchman's Bar Park near Vancouver, Washington. In 2007, a partnership between Confluence, Washington State University's Vancouver satellite campus, and the Port of Ridgefield agreed to move the proposed center to the Ridgefield waterfront. The 40-acre location had been placed on the federal Superfund list a decade earlier after Pacific Wood Treating, a commercial wood preservative facility, declared bankruptcy and abandoned the site. The company left behind a toxic mix of chlorinated solvents, petroleum hydrocarbons (also known as PCBs or "forever chemicals"), and dioxin. Confluence's environmental research center was part of a larger plan to remediate the site and redevelop the waterfront. ("Confluence Project Records—Archives West" 2018, Box 4, Folder 44) The center's focus was to be the health and sustainability of the Columbia River, its dynamic, endangered ecosystems, and its Indigenous histories. Design proposals and blueprints drafted for the facility would include a visitor's pavilion, theater, and lecture hall. The 2008 financial crisis and the ensuing Great Recession drained the budgets of the partner organizations, and plans for the research center were halted.

The number "7" is crucial to understanding the Confluence Project and its attitude toward the environment and sustainability. The Seven Generations concept is a philosophical and ethical exercise foundation to many Native American Indigenous cultures. It is most frequently associated with the Haudenosaunee (Iroquois) tribe of the northeastern part of what is now Canada and the United States. It states that decisions made in the present will affect the lives of our descendants seven generations from now. The concept is nonlinear in that it also asks us to reflect on how the decisions made by our own ancestors seven generations ago are impacting our current moment. (Natcher, Walker, and Jojola 2013) There are seven Story Circles at Sacajawea State Park. Petroglyphs and pictographs throughout the Columbia Gorge are often clustered in groups of seven or contain other allusions to the number. Lin has spoken about the Indigenous

DOI: 10.4324/9781003309024-7

concept of the seven sacred directions: the four cardinal directions (north, south, east, west), above, below, and in, or center. Each location's design reinforces the concept by encouraging visitors to pay attention to what we see on the ground, in the air, and all around us. Awareness of our location in space and our sur-roundings is central to human perceptual experience and identify, but occurs most often at an unconscious or habitual level. Lin's installations invite visitors to be attentive to those same surroundings, to bring into conscious awareness the deliberate decisions made over the past two centuries to co-create our dam-aged planet and imagine a better world seven generations from now. Seven is also an important, even mystical number across historical eras and cultures. Its recurrence within the Confluence Project, although indebted to Indigenous beliefs, is another example of how Lin recognizes the familiarity and intercon-nection between different cosmologies and ways of understanding the world.

It was clear from the beginning that the Celilo site would be both logistically challenging and emotionally charged. Celilo Park rests on sacred tribal lands and the inundation of Celilo Falls is still an open wound. Any construction at the location risks disturbing archeologically sensitive artifacts. Lin herself acknowl-edged the perils of attempting to build here in an address at the Portland Art Mu-seum in 2004: "I think for me Celilo will talk about loss, but again the loss has been—as we've talked to different tribes—so hard to bear, in a way so painful at times that it might be a site that is left in concept and in word and it is the debate and the discussion that takes place over it that becomes as much a part of that art." ("Confluence Project Records—Archives West" 2018, 2018_021_077) For over 10,000 years, Celilo Falls, located near The Dalles, Oregon, was an important center for trade, fishing, and spiritual practice. Indigenous groups from the Co-lumbia River Plateau and beyond gathered there to fish the annual salmon runs. In 1957, the construction of The Dalles Dam inundated the falls, and the fish-ing site was destroyed. Lin's plans include the construction of a curving cantile-vered bridge or walkway that overlooks the now-inundated waterfalls Figure 6.1. The walkway will begin at a visitor's pavilion that will list endangered and ex-tinct species. Inside the pavilion, a historical recording of the roaring falls will be looped during daylight hours. A carved basalt handrail in the shape of the Colum-bia will connect the pavilion to the walkway, which gradually curves out over the river, creating a 180-degree view of the site and its surroundings.

Plans were approved by the four tribes with treaty rights to Celilo Falls—Yakama, Nez Perce, Umatilla, and Warm Springs. In February 2019, however, then Yakama Chairman, JoDe Goudy, withdrew tribal support of Lin's project in a letter to the U.S. Army Corps of Engineers. The letter states that develop-ment of the park "risks further destruction of the Yakama Nation's cultural resources." (Phinney 2019) Both Lin and the Army Corps of Engineers have refused to proceed without consent from all of the tribes. Confluence Project Director, Colin Fogarty, views the site's unbuilt status not as a failure but as a moment "to reflect and listen respectfully. Our guiding principles for moving forward are to listen first to our tribal partners and respect all voices along the

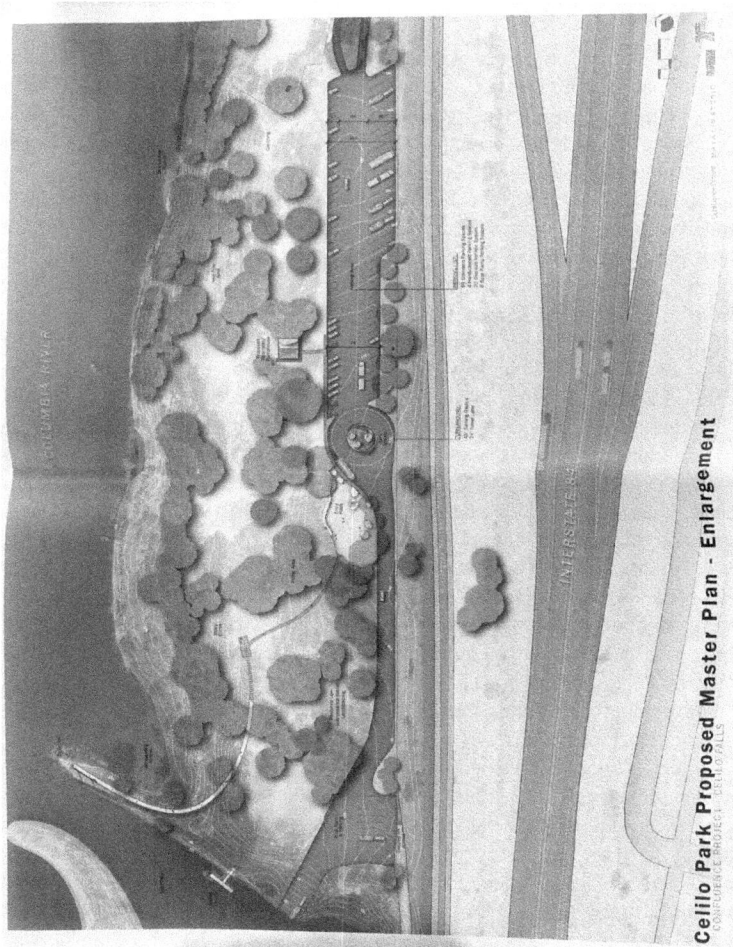

Figure 6.1 Celilo Park Proposed Master Plan, May 2012. Unbuilt. The image includes
modifications for the parking lot, Entry Pavilion, Story Circle, and Celilo
Arc in upper-left corner.

Sources: Box 7, Folder 1. WCMss444. Confluence Project Records. Whitman College and Northwest Archives.

Columbia River." Lin's statement above acknowledges the further emotional
and spiritual anguish additional building at Celilo Park might elicit. It should
also preempt an interpretation of the inability to complete seven physical sites
as a kind of failure of the overall vision.

Confluence in the Classroom

There are other less material and quantifiable manifestations of Confluence that should be considered alongside the earthworks and installations. Confluence in the Classroom was created to bring Native American art and culture education into schools. In the early 2000s, 12 schools in the Pacific Northwest submitted proposals to the Confluence Project for collaborative, student-driven art pieces that would build on the work Lin began. The selected schools received a $5000 grant to fund these initiatives. Confluence in the Classroom also provided resources for educators to connect their students with Indigenous artists and visit culturally significant sites that could be incorporated into future class curricula. Lillian Pitt, Toma Villa, and other Native artists of the Northwest region created hands-on workshops to help students make lasting art projects for their respective campuses Figure 6.2. The results were often dazzling. A mural project at Discovery Middle School in Vancouver, Washington, introduced students to "Ichishkin," the language and culture of a number of Plateau and River tribes was part of a year-long course of study at Lyle Secondary School. Wishram School near the Yakama and Warm Springs Reservations created a "documentary installation project and fabric mural" addressing contemporary issues of urban Native identity at the Native American Youth and Family Center in Portland. ("Confluence Project Records—Archives West" 2018, Boxes 11 and 12) Since retitled Confluence in the Schools, the program to further its mission beyond the original cycle of grant-funded projects, connected students to Native land through residencies, field trips, professional development, collaborations, and the Confluence Library. Innovative course curricula designed for schools at the K-12 level are another such example of Confluence's dialogical dimensions.

Likewise, the Confluence Project website should not be viewed simply as a promotional resource. It also acts as an archive, providing ongoing engagement with broader issues associated with the Columbia River Plateau. It features repositories of historical documentation alongside video clips of tribal elders and leaders. A page dedicated to the site at Sacajawea State Park features an introductory video with moving interviews by Wifrid "Scotty" Scott (Nez Perce) and Antone Minthorn (CTUIR) talking about the history of the location, its importance for trade between tribal groups, and its ecology. In 2022, Confluence published the first issue of *Voices from the River*, a journal devoted to the organization's ongoing mission to foreground Indigenous stories.

Confluence's value may ultimately reside not in the physical installations themselves but in the less tangible yet still transformative immaterial encounters and exchanges like those cited here. On a warm, early evening in the fall of 2022, the Pacific Northwest History Conference held its closing event at Sacajawea State Park. A panel entitled "Rabbits and Rivers: An Evening of Language, Stories, and River Memories" featured a group of Indigenous scholars gathered informally near the Seasonal Rounds circle

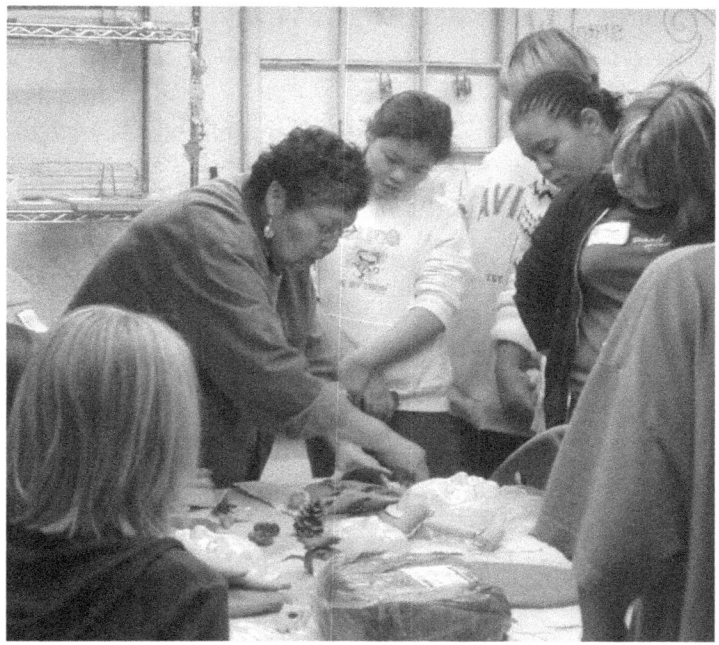

Figure 6.2 Lillian Pitt working on an art project with students at Grace Academy in Portland, Oregon, ca. 2005. Photographer Unknown. This educational outreach was part of "The Confluence Project in the Schools" program, later called "Confluence in the Classroom."

Sources: Confluence 2018-021-31. WCMss444. Confluence Project Records. Whitman College and Northwest Archives.

and the refurbished cultural center. At one point, historian Laurie Arnold and moderator Emily Washines responded to an audience question about laughter. Arnold discussed her research into George Wright's attack on Columbia Plateau peoples after Colonel Edward Steptoe's defeat at the Battle of Tohotonimme. Washines reminded the audience that Palouse, Spokane, and Coeur d'Alene tribes banded together after the US Army had attacked Native women. Wright was enraged at Indian's laughter and joyous customs around eating, games, and fishing that he had observed in large gatherings. Washines spoke about the US soldiers going into the mountains to "finish the job," only to be met with the laughter of Indians who had vanished into the hills. The soldiers were unable to fight or follow in the darkness of a foreign territory. Very little was said about Lin or the artwork that evening. Instead, the spaces were animated by the robust, lively conversation that brought new stories to light.

References

"Confluence Project Records—Archives West." 2018. WCMss.444-2018-021. Whitman College and Northwest Archives. https://archiveswest.orbiscascade.org/ark:/80444/xv285430

Natcher, David C., Ryan Walker, and Theodore S. Jojola. 2013. "Reclaiming Indigenous Planning." In *McGill-Queen's Native and Northern Series 70*. Montreal; Kingston: McGill-Queen's University Press.

Phinney, Wil. 2019. "Yakama Decision Halts Celilo Art Project." *Confederated Umatilla Journal* 27 (2): 20–21.

Conclusion

In August of 2022, artist Michael Heizer's City was finally opened to the public after 50 years. Its construction was shrouded secrecy. City is a monumental earthwork located in a remote area of the Nevada desert, several hours from Las Vegas. Its exact location remains a mystery. Even in an era of satellite mapping, Heizer has managed to obscure its geographical coordinates and limit publicity. City consists of several "complexes," or large stone and concrete architectural forms that recall Minimalist sculptures of the 1960s and 1970s, a style and period with which Heizer is most frequently associated. The entire work spans nearly one-half mile. Towering, angular, geometric shapes rise from the desert floor, evoking a strange synergy between his gallery installations and the temples of ancient Egyptian and Mayan civilizations. Much of the discourse about City emphasizes Heizer's interest in archeology. His father, Robert Heizer, was well-known in the field and brought his son on research trips and digs as a boy. A lengthy profile of the artist published in the *New Yorker* in 2016 details this history, making explicit the connections between archeological practice, ancient civilization and ritual, and the carefully crafted aura of mystery surrounding City.

A number of things stand out when assessing Heizer's project. It is spectacular. Photographs of the site emphasize its monumentality and the remote "emptiness" of its location. Surrounded by distant desert mountains and sagebrush, the massive sculptured hills and protruding, trapezoidal towers make for instantly appealing visual imagery. If the earthworks have a specific function, the artist has yet to reveal it. Observatory? Funerary? Ritualistic? Symbolic? Heizer isn't saying. Articles and publicity about City reinforce its inscrutability by emphasizing that he has been working alone on the project, in the desert, with only rudimentary tools. (Pictures or descriptions of modern building technologies are consistently eschewed.) This is strictly a one-man production.

The deliberate framing of Heizer's work evokes many of the most sacred tropes about the Great Works of Art: they are products of a singular authorial vision, a culminating Masterpiece from one of the twentieth century's seminal sculptors, working with and against Nature to achieve his dream, battling

DOI: 10.4324/9781003309024-8

bloated bureaucracies that sought to sabotage the project by building a railway to carry nuclear waste to nearby Yucca Mountain. Heizer's project similarly reinscribes the mythologies of the West and Manifest Destiny. The barren landscape of the surrounding desert is the tabula rasa, the unblemished canvas, awaiting Heizer's civilizing genius.

Critiques of City appeared almost immediately, noting the problematic association between so-called empty Western spaces and the history of settler colonialism. "The artist's earthen voids seem to unintentionally analogize the absence of the land's Native peoples by echoing the forms of mass graves and mines, two sides of the same extractive process of colonization that fueled so much of the settlement of Nevada and other western territories and created the conditions of emptiness which Heizer is so fond of," writes Chris Fernald in the art blog *hyperallergic*. (Bishara and Fernald 2022) Terms like "empty" and "barren" obfuscate the histories of America's Indigenous populations, while the mystification of City's purpose and its association with ancient monoliths render those same histories as distant relics of the past. Indigenous artist Raven Chacon was more forceful in her critique, stating: "…that's what we're looking at: people replacing those that were displaced with their own monuments." (Liu 2022)

Photographs of City as it slowly opened to the media and small, select artworld individuals show spaces devoid of any kind of living presence, human or nonhuman. This city is entirely depopulated. To look at images of City is to be reminded of the monoliths and dystopias of 1970s era science fiction sets. Where once the futuristic movies of Stanley Kubrick or the art design of Douglas Trumbull took its cue from Minimalism's basic geometric shapes and industrially fabricated surfaces, Heizer returns the favor by making a contemporary set on which those films might be remade. City's complexes look like landing strips for UFOs. ("Triple Canopy – Star Wars: A New Heap by John Powers" 2008)

If Heizer's project is a monument whose mystery is forever shrouded, Lin's Confluence Project created a counter-monument. She did not build statues to heroic explorers. She created living spaces that reinvigorate histories from multiple perspectives. The earthworks of Confluence share the stories of the Columbia River, not as an obstacle to be overcome in order to make trade, expansion, and growth easier for a new nation. The river systems of the Snake and Columbia were, and are, living providers of food, culture, travel, and commerce. They sustain life not just for humans but for the countless species that depend on a healthy ecosystem—a system in danger of collapse. Where Heizer's work is remote, the Confluence Project is accessible. Where City reifies the concept of artist as mad genius, Lin's earthworks are dependent on collaboration and community. Because each Confluence site is situated on public, yet archeologically sensitive lands, their construction required input from a staggering list of federal, state, and local government agencies.

Lin's lifelong interest in the environment also meant that sites were chosen for their ecological value. For example, Cape Disappointment is not only the endpoint of the Corps of the Discovery's westward expedition, it is also the place where the Columbia meets the Pacific Ocean. This vital estuary is home to coastal tribes and a transit point for salmon—a unique habitat for this anadromous species, one of the few that can exist in both salt and freshwater. Salmon are both a fundamental food source for all tribal communities of the Pacific Northwest and inland Plateau and a foundational cultural touchstone. Life revolves around and with this once-abundant species. Similarly, the confluence of the Snake and Columbia Rivers outside of Pasco, Washington, was a crucial point of contact for Plateau peoples, a meeting place, a place for trade and communication, games and negotiations, and sharing of stories, rituals, and traditions for over 10,000 years.

Heizer's City and the Confluence Project differ in their respective attitudes toward the environment. If, as I have said, Heizer's mounds and complexes evoke a dystopian future devoid of life, it is impossible not to read it as a bleak commentary about the climate crisis and the collapse of biodiversity, of which we are subject to new and ever-more frightening examples in the daily news. I suppose a generous interpretation of City might argue that Heizer's work is a cautionary tale. Perhaps City posits an attempt to avoid turning the world into depopulated ruins? But Heizer has always been an artist with the mind of a real estate developer. The monochromatic publicity photographs circulating in art journals instead evoke gravelly, carless parking lots or drought-stricken golf courses. The jutting, cantilevered trapezoids and standing, upside-down L-shaped outcroppings look like ventilation ducts for nuclear fallout shelters or a billionaire's bunker safehouse designed to wait out society's collapse. Heizer's City is a tech-bro Accelerationist's wet dream.

Lin's body of work has always taken a different attitude toward its immediate surrounding environment. Even her iconic Vietnam Veteran's Memorial could be said to be environmental in that it is situated in a manner as to make the federal buildings that surround it part of the work. The famously polished black granite is a reflective surface, a mirror that forces viewers to see themselves in the loss represented by the wall of names. Beginning in the 1990s, her work became more overtly environmental, or perhaps it is better to say that the environment, ecology, habitats, and systems of life that sustain being, all became the explicit subject and subject matter of her work. Pieces like *Groundswell* (1992–1993) and the *Wave Field* series (1995–2008) address how humans envision, interact with, and alter the natural world, thereafter becoming the dominant focus of her career as a visual artist. The Confluence Project began as a way to tell the larger story of how Lewis and Clark's expedition provided an inflection point for the transformation of the environment in ways that would benefit settler colonists: dispossession, claiming and partitioning of land, the exploitation of natural resources, the mining of precious metals, and the use of existing or modified river systems as transit arteries for goods and people. The list goes on. Early promotional literature emphasizes how the works would integrate environmental concerns and history with an awareness of and sensitivity to the tremendous changes the journey of Lewis and Clark effected on Native Americans and their homelands.

Each site serves as a reminder of the customs and rituals that allowed human beings to coexist in relative harmony with nature. From honoring the First Foods ceremonies of the Plateau peoples to documenting the various species in and around the Columbia River Gorge listed in William Clark's journals, alongside their current status (endangered, extinct), Lin's approach to connecting viewers with their surroundings is not based on a nostalgia for what has been lost. Instead, each Confluence site asks us to recognize history's sedimentation by also seeing what exists in these locations *currently*. Taken together, the winding paths, inscribed walkways, amphitheaters, shelters, bridges, and outlooks all command a total bodily and sensory engagement with each location. The sites deliberately incorporate the iconography of industrialization. The barges, jettys and boat docks, the sounds and smells of heavily trafficked highways, electrical towers, parking lots and bathrooms, abandoned farm equipment, and grain silos, become anthropogenic earthworks themselves. Such infrastructure tends to render itself invisible in juxtaposition to art in public places. Lin's earthworks are characterized by appealing and thoughtful landscaping and riparian restoration. The Confluence Project also asks us to see contemporary human interventions of all kinds alongside our imaginary reconstructions of Lewis and Clark's expedition. This kind of temporal dislocation, a form of unsettled viewing, also has a future-oriented purpose. If the Corps of Discovery voyage occurred roughly seven generations ago, Confluence asks us to consider a world seven generations from now. This speculative projection is an attempt to retrain viewers to look beyond our presentist way of life. Seeing a sustainable world approximately 200 years from now is something we absolutely must do. Lin's work is a call to action, to circle back to William Fox's quote in the introduction.

At the time of this writing, it seems unlikely that the plans for the installation at Celilo Park will move forward. If so, Lin's artworks along the Columbia River may be complete with five physical locations, not the original seven, as planned. Whether there are five earthworks, or six, or seven as the initial plans called for, Confluence should not be judged for what is left unbuilt but for the work that continues. From the outset, Confluence was dedicated to doing community and educational outreach, both about Lin's earthworks as well as the history of Native American cultures in the Pacific Northwest. Since the completion of the most recently built site at Chief Timothy Park, the Confluence organization has pivoted to foregrounding the voices and histories of Native American communities and helping to maintain and conserve the art installations. The nonprofit continues its community and educational outreach in the form of public programming. They maintain a robust website that highlights the artworks, announces upcoming events, and archives past lectures and panels. They have also launched a journal. Lin herself once spoke of writing her own book about Confluence. That too, she has said, might be considered its own "site." These immaterial activities and functions expand the physicality of Confluence in ways that cannot be quantified but that will yield immeasurable qualitative differences to the lives of those who experience them.

One final point of comparison with City is worth exploring: the issue of spectacle and its relation to contemporary public sculpture. Heizer's work, as I have discussed, will be most widely experienced through photographs of its monumental mounds and forms, all of which emphasize the vastness of the work within the even more vast confines of an inhospitable-looking desert basin. The spectacle of City stands in sharp contrast to the Confluence Project. Reconnecting the Klickitat Trail via a pedestrian bridge is of immense symbolic value. Viewers, however, have been trained to overlook those objects that do not announce themselves as special or unique, or that blend in more easily with the scenery. A grove of dead cedar trees, an amphitheater, and a series of basalt rings that might easily pass for large planters without the engraved pictographs or accompanying signage are subtle, quiet, reflective markers that urge us to expand our consciousness and awareness beyond the objects themselves. This is not a process human beings are accustomed to performing in a world that values an aesthetic experience of immediacy, glamour, and beauty—but a specific kind of beauty, one that attracts and holds the eye, that "pops" and wows and provides instant gratification. That the various sites of Confluence do not perform this function, or do not perform it in the same way, can make it a more "difficult" work to understand in relation to something like Heizer's City. Confluence's deliberate rejection of spectacle may also be the very quality that accounts for a lack of awareness about it. This book hopes to remedy that issue.

Overlooking Confluence is also a way of continuing to ignore and avoid the painful histories of genocide and dispossession of which Lewis and Clark's expedition was a precursor. A work that asks us to confront the environmental consequences of two centuries of "injecting carbon dioxide into the atmosphere" (Mitchell 2013, 6) and to consider the impact of industrialized pollution on humans and nonhumans alike is unlikely to make the art tourism bucket list. While this attitude is explainable, even understandable, it is also the very quality that makes Confluence so urgent. Our collective, willful inability to confront the climate crisis is a direct result of our desire for distraction and spectacle. Will we recover from this telos, this Death Drive? How can we encounter the world differently and experience humanity's impact on nonhuman species more expansively? Confluence provides methods for recovery and reinvention. Is it already too late?

References

Bishara, Hakim, and Chris Fernald. 2022. "Michael Heizer's Empty Empire." Hyperallergic. Accessed September 26, 2022. http://hyperallergic.com/764254/michael-heizers-empty-empire/

Liu, Jasmine. 2022. "What Do Native Artists Think of Michael Heizer's New Land Art Work?" Hyperallergic. Accessed September 21, 2022. http://hyperallergic.com/763203/what-do-native-artists-think-of-michael-heizers-new-land-art-work/

Mitchell, Timothy. 2013. *Carbon Democracy: Political Power in the Age of Oil.* London: Verso.

"Triple Canopy—Star Wars: A New Heap by John Powers." 2008, Triple Canopy. Accessed October 19, 2023. https://tc3.canopycanopycanopy.com/contents/star_wars__a_new_heap

Index

For Product Safety Concerns and Information please contact our EU
representative GPSR@taylorandfrancis.com
Taylor & Francis Verlag GmbH, Kaufingerstraße 24, 80331 München, Germany